MW01122036

Jesus and Red Sox Nation

How the Story of the Red Sox Fits in the Bigger Story of Life

MIKE LAIRD

Copyright © 2013 Mike Laird

Published in Upton, MA by Every Square Inch Publishing.

All rights reserved. Written permission must be secured from the publisher or author to use or reproduce any part of this book except for brief quotations in critical reviews or articles.

All Bible readings taken from *The Message* unless otherwise noted.

ISBN: 0615905471
ISBN-13: 978-0615905471

DEDICATION

This book is dedicated to all those who just don't seem to fit in when it comes to church and religion. May the God of all good things, including baseball, open you up to a spirituality not based on knowing the rules but on knowing the Creator behind it all.

CONTENTS

ACKNOWLEDGMENTS

Special thanks to Deborah Thomas for the encouragement and amazing editing help she brought to this project. Thanks also to Gretchen Neff Lambert for her cover design contribution, Ken White for his incredible optimism, and Joe Castiglione and Dave O'Brien for years of great Red Sox broadcasting. I felt nudged by God to write this book… it's now up to him!

INTRODUCTION

What in the world do Red Sox Nation and Jesus really have in common? Come on, is this book serious? Good questions. Let me start by saying that this book is not a theological work or an academic dissertation or comic musings. It's not a lot of things but it is serious. By looking at the similarities, common themes, struggles and victories of Red Sox Nation alongside the life mission and message of Jesus, I believe we just might come to understand and appreciate both even more. The first chapter, God and Baseball, lays a foundation for the relevancy of God in sports. The next six takes us on a tour of how Jesus and Red Sox Nation can enhance the understanding of each other. In chapter 5, Reversing the Curse, the similarities are striking and I think you will develop a better appreciation both for what Jesus did and for what the Red Sox did in their climactic 2004 season. In the end, I hope by reading this book two things will happen for you: one, your affections for Red Sox Nation will be heightened; and two, you will have a deeper understanding and appreciation of Jesus.

Each chapter is laid out like an inning in baseball. The top of the inning focuses on some aspect of Red Sox Nation, while the bottom half gives Jesus his opportunity at bat.

What's more, the book is set up somewhat like the historic 2004 AL Championship series against the Yankees. It begins slowly (hopefully not as shaky as the Sox's first 3 games of that series), building on each chapter until you reach the dramatic "Reverse of the Curse" chapter, finishing a little less dramatically but hopefully as triumphantly as the ensuing sweep of St. Louis which ended Boston's 86-year World Series Championship drought. So start from the beginning, it will make the rest of the book that much better.

Also, at the end of each chapter, I've included "Between Innings," a section with questions to help you get the most out of the reading. Think of it as warming up between innings. I highly recommend exploring Between Innings with a friend. After all, isn't almost anything better when shared?

1. GOD AND BASEBALL:
The Citgo sign as sacred guidepost

Growing up, I heard warnings in church about not making sports your "idol."   In other words, don't love sports more than you love God. For kids, that's hard to understand. The tangible joy of a neighborhood pick-up game with friends in the back yard or a vacant lot is hard to beat. Maybe that's why the movie "The Sandlot" (1993) is still so popular. It captures the highs and lows, the thrills of victory and the agonies of defeat that accompany any ordinary day of neighborhood ball. With one swing, of the bat you could become the hero or the "goat." One ninth inning clutch hit would redeem any previous strikeouts or fly balls dropped. God, on the other hand, is hard to get a handle on. He's invisible! He's intangible. You can read about what he is like but you can never really picture him. Depending on your particular experience with church, God may have seemed more like someone to be afraid of than someone to love more than sports.

I have more than one over obsessed sports fan in my family who, if sports can be an idol, has made it one. For the sake of the illustration, let's name that relative Cousin John. Maybe you have an uncle, cousin, brother or father like Cousin John. Depending on the season, I can resemble Cousin John myself. Here are some telltale signs of being like him. When baseball or football (or whatever other sport) season hits, you begin to eat, drink, and sleep that sport. You become THE unofficial expert on your favorite team; watching every game, memorizing every stat, and reading every newspaper article. You can't rest with just the basic knowledge of your team; after all, how can you defeat an opponent you don't know? So, soon after opening day, you become as proficient in opposing team stats as any TV commentator. In fact, you may even catch the analysts in an error from time to time. But it doesn't stop there! Next thing you know, you're buying hats, T-shirts, and bumper stickers. You're getting updates of your favorite team on your smart phone and have an Internet window forever open on your desktops at work and home. The icing on the cake comes when you turn your basement to be a full-scale, officially licensed, sports bar furnished with recliners, leather couches, and the ubiquitous "Dogs Playing Poker" painting.

At this point you might ask, "Come on, is this really such a bad thing? Everyone has a passion, a hobby, right?" The only way to answer that question, the only way to discern if sports have really become your idol, is to interview your spouse, children or closest friends. Ask them if they feel valued, appreciated, or loved by you. Tell them you're willing to do any one thing for them that is in your ability to do and see what they say. If the answer is "Spend more time with me" or "Please care about the things I like for a change" then you might want to take a second look at your favorite team or sport in light of your closest relationships.

My point in all this is not to make us feel bad about loving sports. Actually, I want to do the opposite. Unless you're hurting the ones you love most by your obsession, the love of sports can actually help you better love God and the life that God has given you. Let me explain before you close this book for good.

God has often been misrepresented, painted as a cosmic judge or divine policeman just waiting for us to screw up so he can give us what we deserve. Few people think of God as the giver of sunsets, beauty, intelligence and all other good things including, yes, baseball. It wasn't until my college days that I realized that everything good, no matter how secular it may seem, has God's fingerprints all over it. Think of the times you have been awed by creation. Maybe it was during a walk on an empty beach or a breathtaking view from a mountaintop or an incredible sunset or starry night from your own backyard. Whatever the scenario, something stirred within you a sense of peace, a sense of wonder, a sense of something bigger than yourself. That something, I believe, was the Creator speaking through his creation.

It doesn't just happen in nature. It happens everywhere in life. Have you ever listened to a song that either just relaxed you and gave you a sense of peace or pumped you up and made you feel alive and passionate, like anything's possible?

Or maybe it was a movie that grabbed your heart and for a moment caused you to rise above your own situation and feel what life could be like as the hero. These experiences all point to a greater peace, a greater satisfaction, and a greater hero. We can experience it even in something as simple as a good meal. After tasting the perfectly tender, perfectly roasted bite of prime rib, your mouth and mind wants to shout out, "man that was incredible". The fact that we were created with the right mix and abundance of taste buds so that we can fully enjoy even the most mundane tasks as chewing is a signal directing our attention toward the One who created us for that pleasure. Everywhere, in art, music, film, nature, and yes, in sports there are guideposts pointing us to God. These guideposts help us to see beyond our circumstances and glimpse a bit of God's extraordinary reality in the midst of our ordinary lives. A famous theologian, Abraham Kuyper, once said, "In the total expanse of human life there is not a single square inch of which Jesus Christ does not declare, 'That is mine!'" If he were still alive today, I think Kuyper would agree that baseball is no exception.

Once you recognize God's hand is in every area of life, anything and everything becomes charged with new meaning. Seeing a baby smile or walk for the first time, having a great conversation with friends, and witnessing David Ortiz knock one out of the park to seal another win for the Red Sox spark in us something greater than our normal run of the mill emotions; something that hasn't come out in us in a while or maybe ever. That's why people shout till they're hoarse at concerts, why people cry while watching a movie, and why

38,000 fans jump out of their seats in elation as Papi slams another one over the Green Monster. Something stronger, more courageous, more passionate, more generous, more heroic is stirred within us, pointing us to bigger and better possibilities. In essence, pointing us to the life we have always wanted, the life God has designed us to have and ultimately, pointing us to God himself, the author and sustainer of all this.

You might be thinking at this point, "Okay, but how does Jesus fit into all of this?" Good question. I think the Bible can shed some light here. Let's look at what the apostle Paul wrote in his letter to a young church in the New Testament:

"We look at this Son (Jesus) and see the God who cannot be seen. We look at this Son and see God's original purpose in everything created. For everything, absolutely everything, above and below, visible and invisible, rank after rank after rank of angels—everything got started in him and finds its purpose in him. He was there before any of it came into existence and holds it all together right up to this moment." ~ Colossians 1:15-17

This is a pretty heavy theological statement but the big idea is actually pretty simple. What this Bible reading is saying is that Jesus was right there from the start of existence and has his hand in creating and sustaining all of existence. Whenever we think of creation we always think of God the Father, like the Michelangelo painting where God is reaching out for Adam. Our Bible reading tells us that Jesus was there from the get go assisting in creation. It's funny that when we think of Jesus we usually just consider Christmas (his birth) and Easter (his death and resurrection). We never think of what Jesus does before and after his time on earth. This reading lets us know that Jesus, somehow, in the mystery of the Trinity, is co-creating with God.

"Whoa, whoa, whoa," you might be thinking, "that's great but how can a baseball game, or a baby's smile or a walk on the beach be pointers to Jesus?" Our Bible reading starts off by telling us that Jesus is at the source of everything. He was the Master Designer who mulled over the blueprints of creation giving everything special meaning and purpose.

Take laminin for example. Laminin is a protein in our body that holds our skin and all our organs in place. It is literally the glue of the human body and it happens to taken on the shape of a cross (try searching for 'Laminin' on Google or Wikipedia)[1].

I can't prove the existence of God just because 'human glue' at a molecular level resembles the shape of the cross. But I can say that even at the molecular level there are hints of Christ. It's an incredible coincidence that the material that holds the human body together takes the form of a cross, the symbol of Christ's love and sacrifice that holds all creation together. As it says in our reading, "everything got started in him and finds its purpose in him. He was there before any of it came into existence and holds it all together right up to this moment".

---

[1] Although I am no medical scientist, I checked laminin out on wikipedia.org (and other medical scientific websites) and it appears to be legit. Cf Louie Giglio's How Great Is Our God talk.

Let's take a more ordinary example: a baby's smile. I remember a special moment some years back when my youngest child was only three months old. I was playing on the living room rug with my daughter, Phoebe. She was lying on a blanket and I was talking and singing to her. I wish I could convey to you the largeness of her smile and the brightness of her eyes as she watched me. Enamored by my little girl, I said to my wife Laura, "Isn't it amazing how she looks at you as if you're the greatest thing in the universe." Then, without thinking at all about this chapter, I blurted out, "It's almost as if God is using her to love us." A baby's smile, just one of the billion pointers that are whispering, "There is something more, something bigger."

When we begin to see baseball in this light, going to Fenway Park with your friends or with your kids can becomes sort of a sacred ritual. If rituals are events that connect people with God, then recognizing God at the ball park should qualify as one. When we recognize that the fun and excitement of jumping out of your seat when Jacoby Ellsbury steals another base is rooted in how God designed us and what he wants for us, then we can appreciate our life, our world and our faith all the more. You've probably experienced the almost reflexive jump to your feet when your hometown hero stares down a 100 mph fastball and then knocks it out of the park to seal the victory. If you were to pause for a second to acknowledge the spark of joy inside you at that moment and later think about your reaction, you may find yourself at the Creator's doorstep. In theory, even the Citgo sign can be a sacred guidepost pointing us to God!

If you've ever been to the place where they make Louisville Slugger baseball bats, you can't miss the colossal, "God-sized" bat that leans against and towers above the factory building. When I first saw this, I envisioned the company saying, "Let's let the ONE who gave us the mind, ability, and heart to play baseball, take a turn at  bat." Faith and baseball are not mutually exclusive. I think both can enhance the other.

That is why this book is serious. The idea that something so real, so fabric-of-America as Red Sox Nation can illuminate, elevate, and more importantly help us identify with something so immense as the life and ministry of Jesus is powerful. More importantly, even if there's just a possibility that God exists and has made himself known through the person of Jesus, then getting to know and understand who Jesus is and what he did has immense value. And what better way to explore that possibility than through lens of Red Sox Nation?

BETWEEN INNINGS:

1) What parts of your life bring you the most joy (fishing, watching the game with friends, a mountain top view, etc.)?

2) What is it about that experience that makes it so enjoyable?

3) What are some ways in which that experience might be a guidepost to God?

2. THE BOSTON ATTITUDE:
A different way of life

I was two years into my marriage, 24 years old, and had just finished a 15-hour road trip. We drove a fully packed, 16-ft. rental truck from Boston to Hudsonville, Michigan. Hudsonville, known as the salad bowl of West Michigan because it grew lettuce, carrots, onions, etc., was a tiny farming town just outside Grand Rapids. Tired and hungry, we pulled into a little pizza joint about two miles away from the home we would be renting for the year while I finished up grad school. I just wanted an ice cold Coke and a nice Greek-style pizza. I soon discovered from the quizzical looks at the counter that they weren't familiar with the term "Greek pizza" in the Midwest! So we ordered our pizza (whatever style), grabbed drinks from the cooler, and sat down at one of the half dozen booths in the shop.

I didn't think I'd have to worry about culture shock. I thought it would be an easy transition since I had married a Mid-westerner from Van Wert, Ohio, another small farming town, and had visited her there a dozen times. I had already learned that people operate at a slower, more relaxed pace. I had been warned about my Boston driving. I was briefed on the rural, small town gossip phenomena. And I had a couple of twilight zone experiences, such as the Walmart clerk remembering I was "the guy from Massachusetts" a whole year after last seeing her. "You must be Laura's friend from Boston," she said as she greeted me at the store entrance. I scratched my head and wondered just how small the town actually was that she could remember me a year later. I gave her the eyebrows up "hi" sign and walked quickly by.

All that to say, I thought I was pretty prepared for the heartland culture shock until the woman sitting on the other side of the pizza place got out of her booth and came over and sat down at ours. Uninvited, with no warning! Where I grew up, that could have been grounds for fighting. I wanted to say, "Hey lady, get out of my booth!" Instead, I muttered a brief "Hiya doing" while I tweaked my eyebrows to let her know I thought the whole thing was weird. Luckily, my very hospitable wife carried the conversation as I tried my best to lighten up and hide my "get out of my space" look.

It was that year, living in Michigan that I could clearly see that New Englanders and especially those of us from eastern Massachusetts[2] are different. In some ways, we're very different. Growing up, I had heard references to a "Boston

[2] I would argue that the closer one is to living inside the 495 beltway (the highway that forms a semicircle around greater Boston) the stronger and more entrenched the Boston attitude is. If you grow up inside the 128 loop (a tighter half-circle even closer to Boston proper), then there's little hope for you.

attitude" in movies or TV programs. Even though I went to an area college (Bentley College in Waltham, MA), I would often hear my out-of-state roommates and friends comment on the attitude. They would usually be talking about it in a denigrating way. We're cold, rude, always in a rush, unemotional, and too private. I remember one professor saying, "New Englanders are very tough to get to know but once you do they're loyal to the core." Despite all this, I still really couldn't see what people were talking about, which I guess shouldn't have surprised me since I was born and raised with "the attitude." It wasn't until that never ending year in West Michigan that I clearly saw the marked difference. We operate on a different wavelength with a different set of unspoken rules and expectations of life. From driving, to relational space, to emotional openness and communication, we just are plainly different than people from other parts of the country. The difference is nicely summed up by that 1990's Budweiser commercial in which the local response to the question, "How ya doing?" was supposed to be something along the lines of, "Good, how you doing?" All the locals respond to the question accordingly. Then, an out-of-stater with a Southern accent walks in and instead of giving the expected answer, he launches into an honest and extended answer about precisely how he's feeling and why.

Another story that highlights this Boston attitude comes from my wife's first holiday experience with my extended family. It was Thanksgiving, we had just gotten engaged and Laura was eager to make a good impression. In Laura's Midwestern family tradition, Thanksgiving is a time of reconnecting with family in more than just superficial ways. It's a time to go deeper into what's going on and how everyone is really doing. In my family tradition, Thanksgiving is notorious for overeating, napping and waking up in time to catch the tail end of a football game. Any gathering of my extended family is always filled with off-color jokes, sarcasm and an endless supply of beer. We talk small talk and pick on those we love most. We never, ever delve below the surface. My wife wasn't ready for this. Thanksgiving Day that year can be summed up by this short conversation Laura and I had in the car driving away from my parents' house that Thanksgiving Day.

Laura: "They hate me!"

Me: "Who hates you?"

Laura: "Your family. No one got to know me. No one engaged me in any meaningful conversations."

Me: "What do you mean? They loved you. They asked you about the car you drive, how much you pay for rent, and where you work. You're in like Flynn!"

Laura (frustrated): "I don't understand your family."

Me (reassuring): "Don't feel bad, neither do I."

When it comes to relationships, Greater Bostonians are different. They say we're more reserved. What that really means is that we aren't in touch with our feelings and frankly, we like it that way[3]. We show you our love and loyalty in actions not in words. We'd enlist in the Army with our best

---

[3] My apologies to all who don't fit this stereotype. I'm sure you're out there; I just didn't grow up with you.

friend just so he doesn't have to go it alone but we'd never put to words our feelings about the relationship. Growing up, the words "I love you" or "I care deeply about you" were in short supply among the men in my family. Those feelings were expressed in other ways. If flowers were on the table it meant Dad screwed up and needed to remind Mom of his love. If my brother wanted to express his love for me he would upgrade the stereo in my car or buy me something. On the other hand, when you screwed up, everyone let you know it. In my family, criticism, often constructive and always laced with a dose of friendly sarcasm, flows like Guinness at Kitty O'Shea's on a Friday night.

When it comes to baseball, local Red Sox fans take this attitude to the game. Everyone one loves to boo an opposing player now and again, but the Boston attitude raises it to a new level. I remember in the mid-90's going to a couple of games against the Oakland A's, sitting in the right field grandstands and hearing fans unceasingly mock Jose Conseco for a string of errors or some bad at bats. The content of those jeers could've made a truck driver blush. Maybe it was Jose's attitude or media presence or waning athletic ability or some domestic abuse allegations that hit the news, whatever it was, Boston fans let Conseco have it when he screwed up. Of course, Jose showed his emotions about the jeering, which made us yell all the more.

Even Red Sox players aren't exempt from the scrutiny of the Boston attitude. The phrase "pulled a Buckner" quickly was coined after the 1986 World Series blooper committed by first baseman Bill Buckner when he let a crucial ground ball roll through his legs into the outfield. The error was the turning point in the game and the series for the Red Sox, prolonging the curse for another 18 years. More than 20 years later, I still hear people say, "He pulled a Buckner."

Luckily, there is a positive side to the Boston attitude. When a player or coach has gained Boston fans' loyalty there is little they can do to lose it. Drew Bledsoe, once the quarterback for the New England Patriots, is a good example of this. Bledsoe's sacrifice and commitment to New England bought him many diehard fans. To this day many New Englanders hold Bledsoe in high regard even though the last half of his football career was very lackluster. Curt Schilling's legendary pitching performance in the 2004 AL Championship series where he wouldn't let a bleeding ankle stop him from pitching is just the kind of thing that buys a player the unquestionable loyalty of a hard to please Boston fan base. Even the subsequent bankruptcy of Shilling's newly founded video game company, 38 Studios, which left the Rhode Island with a $75 million unpaid loan, Schilling, and his bloody sock, still are warmly embraced by the Red Sox Nation fan base. I have heard RI sports fans say the state should have realized Schilling is a baseball player, not a businessman, and the bad debt is Rhode Island's fault.

The Boston attitude promotes a diehard loyalty for Boston players, unless of course that player declines an offer and jumps ship to the Yankees (ahem, Johnny Damon).

How does Jesus fit into this whole scenario? It would be a stretch to say Jesus was emotionally uncommunicative, but long before Boston ever was on the map, Jesus had a call-it-as-you-see-it, in-your-face attitude that equally did not fit into the culture of the day. He had a pre-Boston, Boston attitude. Instead of me trying to convince you of this with my own descriptions, I'm going to let Jesus speak for himself. Here are a few snippets to show you what I mean.

This first piece is taken from the New Testament book of Matthew. Notice the Bostonian-like passion and frankness in Jesus' words and tone of voice (remember Jesus was speaking these words some two thousand years ago):

"You blind guides! You strain out a gnat but swallow a camel. Woe to you, teachers of the law and Pharisees, you hypocrites! You clean the outside of the cup and dish, but inside you are full of greed and self-indulgence. Blind Pharisee! First clean the inside of the cup and dish, and then the outside also will be clean. Woe to you, teachers of the law and Pharisees, you hypocrites! You are like whitewashed tombs, which look beautiful on the outside but on the inside are full of dead men's bones and everything unclean." ~ Matthew 23:24-27

By the intensity and selection of Jesus' words, you might assume he is talking to some social riff-raff or morally corrupt group of people. (It might surprise you to know that Jesus is never harsh with those who don't have their religious act together.) In this reading, Jesus is actually talking to the religious big wigs of his day. They would be the bishops, monsignors, board of trustees, or other church leaders of our time. In Jesus' culture the Pharisees and teachers of the law were not only the religious elite they were also the social elite.

They were very influential religiously, socially, and judicially. They could make your life extremely miserable if you got on their bad side (think Whitey Bulger). To most people they were untouchable. To Jesus, they may as well have been Jose Conseco patrolling right field in an A's uniform. Jesus called it like he saw it.

If you're not familiar with the Bible you might be wondering what got Jesus so upset at these guys. At the heart of Jesus message and mission is the idea of making God accessible to everyone, regardless of social, religious, or economic status. Rich or poor, male or female, insider or outsider, Jesus came to connect people to God. "Seek and save the lost," "proclaim that the Kingdom of Heaven is near," "preach the Good News (or Gospel)" are all ways the Bible uses to say the same thing; that God is not just real but also personal and knowable. This goes for people who think they have their religious act together AND for those who think they never got a chance.

There is a funny Irish prayer that is posted on the wall of many an Irish pub around Boston. It reads,

"May those who love us, love us. And those who don't love us, may God turn their hearts. And if he can't turn their hearts, may he turn their ankles so we will know them by their limping!"

It's a funny prayer intended more for humor than for sacred plea, but I think it is so popular partly because we often think or feel the sentiment behind it. That is, of course, that God is on our side. He's our God, not the God of our idiot co-worker or misfit neighbor. He's on our side not our enemy's side. It's human nature to take this exclusive approach to God. The reality is that God is available to everyone! He hears the prayers of those we love and those we don't. Jesus was so angry because the religious mucky-mucks were holding the people back from experiencing God. Jesus' message is that God is equally available and wanting to connect to everyone, yes, God will embrace even a Yankees fan (now that's grace)!

As a pastor of a church in metro-west Boston, I can't tell you how many times people have come to me expressing frustration with their faith. Most often it boils down to an underlying feeling of not being good enough to be accepted by God or Jesus. It's almost as if God is a cosmic policeman or better yet a divine Santa Claus who has a list he frequently checks and notes who's been bad or good and then doles out punishments and rewards accordingly. There's a Boondocks comic strip by Aaron McGruder that humorously gets at this misconception. In the cartoon strip Riley is trying to clear up his friend Jazmine's confusion between Jesus and Santa Clause:

"See, Santa Claus is a white man somewhere up there who watches you all the time and rewards you if you're good and Jesus is... Uhh... okay, wait, let me start again."

This cartoon does a great job of highlighting how our personal upbringing and viewpoint dictate how we approach and understand Jesus. I grew up in a middle-class Irish Catholic family and, honestly, to me Jesus looked more like the description from the comic strip than the description from the Bible. More importantly, Jesus isn't into legalistic games. Jesus' mission was to help us, good or bad, righteous or not, understand and embrace our Creator.

When it comes to accessibility to God, Jesus' message puts the local hooker on the same plane as the religious elite. Think about that for a minute. This lack of exclusion made Jesus the very antithesis of the religious leadership of his day. And this is why Jesus goes off on the religious elite with such in-your-face passion. They were self-righteously parading around as God's favorites, not only deceiving themselves but keeping the rest of the population from believing that God could ever care about them. So, Jesus gives them a Bostonian-like reality check, helping them see their true, hypocritical, self-righteous selves a little clearer.

One more example of Jesus' pre-Boston, Boston attitude comes from the gospel of Luke, another New Testament book. Let me fill you in ahead of time that Jesus miraculously heals a woman. It would be a very big, newsworthy deal in our day and time. It was equally a big deal in Jesus' day and time. Don't let the crazy response of the synagogue (local Jewish church) leader lead you to believe this happened all the time. It will also help to know that the Sabbath was our version of Sunday. It was a day reserved for church and rest. You couldn't work, travel, do household chores or run errands. Every week the Sabbath was a strictly-observed social and religious holiday! Think of the old Massachusetts Blue Laws and multiply their intensity a hundredfold. Can you guess how Jesus may have rocked the boat? It again sounds a bit like the Conseco ribbing I heard in the right field stands.

"He [Jesus] was teaching in one of the meeting places on the Sabbath. There was a woman present, so twisted and bent over with arthritis that she couldn't even look up. She had been afflicted with this for eighteen years. When Jesus saw her, he called her over. "Woman, you're free!" He laid hands on her and suddenly she was standing straight and tall, giving glory to God.

The meeting-place president, furious because Jesus had healed on the Sabbath, said to the congregation, "Six days have been defined as work days. Come on one of the six if you want to be healed, but not on the seventh, the Sabbath." But Jesus shot back, "You frauds! Each Sabbath every one of you regularly unties your cow or donkey from its stall, leads it out for water, and thinks nothing of it. So why isn't it all right for me to untie this daughter of Abraham and lead her from the stall where Satan has had her tied these eighteen years?"

When he said this, all his opponents were humiliated, but the people were delighted with all the wonderful things he was doing." ~ Luke 13:10-17

The religious elite of Jesus' day, and sadly many in our day, used social status to keep people from fully engaging their faith and added all sorts of legalistic rules to restrict and exclude people. Here, in great Bostonian fashion, Jesus embarrasses the religious leader by showing him that man has misinterpreted God's Sabbath rule, taking it to an asinine degree. Of course God cares more about people than following the rules. As Jesus had said on a different occasion,

"Is the religious law made for people or people for the law?"

Jesus never let the status quo dictate his own actions. He set the standard for authenticity. He didn't let local mucky-mucks intimidate him or hinder him from living out his mission. When it came to the self-righteous religious elite, Jesus called it like he saw it with the frankness and volume of a Red Sox fan. He even had a loyalty streak that resembles Boston sports fans. Do you remember how one of his closest friends and students (St. Peter) denied him three times? Somehow Peter still remained Jesus' solid go-to man, laying a foundation for the early Christian church.

BETWEEN INNINGS:

1) If it were up to the head religious leaders in your town, would you be embraced or excluded at church?

2) In light of Jesus' words in this chapter, what do you think Jesus would say on your behalf?

3) How does that change, in any way, your current posture towards God/Jesus?

3 LOVE THAT DIRTY WATER:
Rising above our circumstances

To understand the average local Boston fan, you have to understand more than just the attitude that makes us rude drivers or critical, skeptical and sarcastic but loyal fans. You have to understand a mentality that goes with it. The Boston Tea Party that helped kick off the American Revolution may have happened over two hundred years ago but New Englanders still have an independent streak a mile wide. In general, we're gritty, proud people that aren't quick to look for a handout but instead make do with whatever we have available. We may not be in touch with our "inner-selves" but when the pressure's on, when it's do or die, we often amaze ourselves and everyone else with what we can accomplish, given the circumstances. I think of it as the 'Dirty Water' mindset. Let me explain.

Ed Cobb wrote the lyrics to and produced a song about Boston called Dirty Water[4]. A song, that some thirty-plus

---

[4] Interestingly enough, all four members of the Standells, the band

years later, captured the hearts of Red Sox fans and became the official theme song of Red Sox Nation. Just as Neil Diamond's Sweet Caroline is played during every eighth inning at Fenway Park, so the Standell's Dirty Water is played at the end of every home game. The lyrics are about the writer's experience with and take on the city of Boston. When trying to figure out what the lyrics mean, it's helpful to know that Cobb was mugged on the Mass Ave bridge (thus, his reference to 'fuggers and thieves'). Here's an unofficial recap of those lyrics:

"I'm gonna tell you a story.

I'm gonna tell you about my town.

I'm gonna tell you a big bad story, baby.

It's all about my town.

Down by the river, down by the banks of the river Charles.

(aw, that's what's happenin' baby)

That's where you'll find me, along with lovers, fuggers, and thieves. (aw, but they're cool people)

Well I love that dirty water. Oh, Boston, you're my home

(oh, you're the number one place)

Frustrated women (I mean they're frustrated)

Have to be in by twelve o'clock (oh, that's a shame)

But I'm wishing and a-hoping, oh that just once those doors weren't locked. Well I love that dirty water. Oh, Boston, you're my home."

I don't know if the author was being sincere or sarcastic, but the song communicates a sense of local pride and ironic

---

that performed the song, had never been to Boston prior to the launch of their one hit wonder.

nostalgia about the bad conditions he experienced while in Boston: being mugged, restrictive curfews, and polluted water. The song gives off a level of love and loyalty for the city that seems disproportionate to his experience. It's as if Cobb were saying sure the streets are unsafe, sure the social atmosphere is lame, sure the water isn't clean, but Boston is the best. This is the "Dirty Water" mindset. It's a "make the most of what you've got, don't need your sympathy, don't want any help," way of thinking. And it's a mindset proliferated by Red Sox Nation.

Unfortunately, the Dirty Water mindset can have some serious negative consequences. Sadly, I have watched more than a couple of friends and relatives go down with their ship because they kept their problems to themselves and were never vulnerable enough to say that small but often impossible to utter four letter word: help. I've witnessed firsthand marriages dissolve (oftentimes without divorce) and friends ruined by debt or forever enslaved by addiction because no one would, or maybe could, bring themselves to ask for help. Although I sometimes find myself in it, I don't advocate this approach. That's what second chances, grace, friends, faith, etc. are for. While the Dirty Water mindset can sometimes cause some heartache, the upside of this way of thinking is that it can bring a stubborn stick-to-it-ness and strength of will that can be very powerful and effective when applied to the right situations.

One example from my younger days, which I still get an occasional ribbing for, comes from a local bike race I entered, called the Tour de Lowell. Although it's not related in any way, shape or form to the racing world's premier event, the Tour de France, this 30-mile bike race through the streets of greater Lowell, Massachusetts, was still a big deal to a 15-year old with high racing aspirations. I was not a huge bicycling enthusiast but for some unexplainable reason, I had visions of grandeur when I entered this race. I was overconfident, undertrained and ill-equipped. While most of the riders had at least somewhat respectable equipment, I was riding on my well-used Huffy ten-speed I got from Caldor's Department Store[5]. This was my first bike race so I had no experience and no real strategy, except to pedal fast. I had heard about 'drafting', when you ride behind someone who shields you from the wind, but I never experienced it or knew how to use it to my advantage. I was just going to ride the greatest race of my life and let the chips fall as they may; and fall they did.

It was a warm and sunny morning in late May. We were all lining up on the cobblestone road in downtown Lowell. They gathered us by skill and age. My friend and I were positioned in the back of the mass of riders. As we were waiting for all the cyclists to be lined up, my friend, Burt Hopkins, looked down to find that he had somehow gotten a flat tire. So, just moments before the start of the race, he had to drop out. Unfazed by the loss of my riding partner, I focused myself on what I hoped to be a brilliant race.

It was brilliant all right. In the excitement of the start, I came out at a pace that was much faster than I could ever sustain. By no means was I in the lead pack, but I was riding

---

[5] Caldor's was the 1980's version of Walmart that wasn't quite able to survive.

with a group of cyclists who were way out of my league. I rode with them for about the first 10 to 15 miles of the race. Because of my inexperience in racing, I didn't realize that part of my success was because I was unknowingly doing a terrific job drafting off this group of riders. The trouble hit when the pack decided to ratchet it up a notch or two, and they began to accelerate to an even faster pace. I kept up with them for about a mile but they soon left me in the dust. I was still trying to pedal at a rate that was way too fast to begin with but now I was without the benefits of drafting.

So, I was approaching the halfway mark of the race riding much faster than I ever anticipated and faster than my dad anticipated. This was a problem because I had only one water bottle. My dad and I picked out a spot at just about the halfway mark where I'd drop my empty bottle and he'd hand me a full one. In theory, it was a great plan, but because I had ridden so fast for so long I passed the mark before my dad reached it. So, there I was, giving it my all with no water for the final 15 miles. To a normal person, this shouldn't have been a problem because we passed so many houses and convenient stores where I could have easily filled up. But the "Dirty Water" attitude reared its ugly head. I was so proud and excited at how well I was riding. I was determined to keep riding the race of my life--with or without water.

As you can imagine, that was foolish. With every mile, my pace slowed. My muscles and mind grew tired. Still, I ground it out, giving everything I had. By the time I reached the finish line, I was borderline delusional. Instead of stopping, I pedaled right through the chutes, pedaling slower and slower until about ¼ mile past the finish. I slowly veered over to the sidewalk, hopped off my bike and blacked out. I'm not sure how long I was out, but I opened my eyes to see my bike lying over me and some bystander waving a hot dog in my face. Embarrassed but starving, I graciously accepted the food, slurped down some water, and my strength slowly returned.

Now, had my dad been there with the water and had I been able to muster up the energy to finish the second half as strong as I had the first, this might have made for a triumphant story. But the Dirty Water mindset doesn't always work the way we want it to.

The New England Patriots might provide a better example than my Tour De Lowell blackout story; specifically, their incredible 2001 season. At the start of the season, no NFL analyst gave New England a chance to make it to the playoffs. They were predicted to have a .500 season at best. With Belichick in his second season as head coach, the Pats were off to a shaky start with a 0-2 record going into the third game of the season. To top it off, with just a few minutes left in their second game, starting quarterback Drew Bledsoe was seriously injured and forced to leave the game. Whatever hope was left for a playoff berth, never mind a Super Bowl win, seemed to evaporate as Bledsoe hobbled off the field. Replacing him would be the young, unheard of, back-up quarterback named Tom Brady who was picked up in the 6th round (199th) in the 2000 draft. Luckily, the Patriots "Loved that Dirty Water" and Brady would go on to lead the Pats to win 11 of their next 14 games--enough to get them into the playoffs. The postseason ended with the Pats upsetting three dumbstruck teams and culminated in a storybook Super Bowl victory.

When the going got tough, the Pats didn't throw a pity party. They were the underdogs heading into almost every game that season, but they didn't let analysts' predictions dictate their mindset. In fact, they kept quiet about everything good and bad, elations and injuries, and simply focused on uniting as a team and winning. For me, one of the more memorable tactics the Pats employed that year happened not during the game but before it, when the players took the field. Instead of coming out individually so the fans can cheer each player separately, which the other NFL playoff teams did back then, they all came out together, introduced only as "the New England Patriots." They didn't look for the sympathy of the media and they didn't make any excuses; they simply counted the cost, worked hard, and delivered.

For those of you in Red Sox Nation born about two decades before me (1973), you might recall the Red Sox's 1967 season as a Dirty Water time. Like the Patriots, the '67 Red Sox were coming off a lackluster year. They had a 72 – 90 record the previous year and were given no chance of going anywhere. Like the Pats' Tom Brady, it was Red Sox's Carl Yastrzemski who came alive with a Dirty Water attitude, powering an unlikely team to win the American League pennant. In the last month of the season (there were no postseason play-offs), Yastrzemski batted an astonishing .421 with 9 home runs and 26 RBIs to help bring the Red Sox to the World Series[6]. The Sox battled it out with the Cardinals, but came up short in Game 7 to lose the series. What started as a very unpromising season ended as one for the history books, just one win shy of a World Series victory. Thanks to the Dirty Water outlook of Yaz and the '67 Sox, it was an incredible season that will be cherished by Red Sox fans for as long as there are fans to recount the stories. Many consider that 1967 season to be the seed of what we now call Red Sox Nation[7].

In 1967, the Red Sox Loved that Dirty Water. In 2001, the New England Patriots Loved That Dirty Water. As I am finishing up this book, the 2013 Red Sox, predicted by almost everyone to be at the bottom of their division have just showed the ultimate expression of Loving that Dirty Water by winning the World Series (but more on that in Chapter 7).

Without a doubt, Jesus also Loved That Dirty Water. On many occasions, Jesus faced incredible odds and had numerous opportunities to back out, make excuses, or take the easy way out. He wasn't surrounded by an all-star cast supporting him. In fact, his students, supporters, and friends were in many ways a rag-tag bunch of outcasts. They were of the unknown, unseasoned, rookie caliber that characterized many of the 2001 Patriots, "Brady Bunch." Still, Jesus did not waiver from his mission. He didn't stop and say "I just

---

[6] Stats from: Yaz's huge summer set the stage in '67. September 18th, 2007 Ian Browne / MLB.com.

[7] The 2007 AL Championship Series is another great example of the Dirty Water mindset. Down by three games the Red Sox muster up three consecutive wins to beat the Cleveland Indians in a great Game 7 finish.

can't take these guys anymore; I quit." He too counted the cost, worked hard, and delivered.

A crystal clear example of this can be seen in Jesus' pre-season warm up better known as the Temptations of Christ. Let's take a look at how Jesus handled the opposition and used a Dirty Water mindset to gain a big exhibition season victory. This event is taken from The Gospel of Matthew, the first of the four accounts of Jesus' life found in the New Testament.

"After fasting forty days and forty nights, Jesus was hungry. The tempter came to him and said, "If you are the Son of God, tell these stones to become bread."

Jesus answered, "It is written: 'Man does not live on bread alone, but on every word that comes from the mouth of God.'"

Then the devil took him to the holy city and had him stand on the highest point of the temple. "If you are the Son of God," he said, "throw yourself down. For it is written: "'He will command his angels concerning you, and they will lift you up in their hands, so that you will not strike your foot against a stone.'"

Jesus answered him, "It is also written: 'Do not put the Lord your God to the test.'"

Again, the devil took him to a very high mountain and showed him all the kingdoms of the world and their splendor. "All this I will give you," he said, "if you will bow down and worship me."

Jesus said to him, "Away from me, Satan! For it is written: 'Worship the Lord your God, and serve him only.'"

Then the devil left him, and angels came and attended him. ~*New International Version*, Matthew 4:2-11

If you're not familiar with the Bible, this excerpt may seem like wild science fiction, like something from a M. Night Shyamalan movie. It probably raised a few questions in your mind like: Did Jesus actually hear or see Satan or did Satan just put those thoughts in Jesus' mind? Was Jesus supernaturally whisked away to the highest point of the temple and mountaintop or did he just have a dream or a vision? These are good questions, but no matter what approach you take when trying to understand this passage, the important thing is that you don't miss the point. Jesus musters up a Dirty Water mindset and without complaint or compromise overcomes the three waves of temptation that Satan uses to try to sideline his mission and ministry before it even starts.

I think it's safe to say that everyone on planet earth believes in the existence of evil. With the incredible, never-ending stories of genocide, homicide, sexual abuse, deception, fraud, corruption, etc. that we read about daily it's very hard to chalk up certain events to poor choices or human nature. Satan, evil personified, however, is a harder leap for some people to make. If you fall into this category, please give the above reading a chance. If you can, suspend your doubts for a moment so you can get the full flavor and value of this event. You might just be surprised at how relevant it is to your own struggles and temptations.

Each of the three temptations is attacking a different human weakness that we can all relate to. The first one is hunger. I don't know if it's my high metabolism rate or my eating habits (I've been on a 'see-food' diet for most of my life; if I see food, I eat it). As, I write this sentence, I am currently very hungry and stuck in a cabin on Martha's Vineyard without a trace of food in sight. I have no car and I'm miles away from the nearest restaurant or store. If I were God incarnate, I wouldn't hesitate to turn a rock, a book, or even some of the cabin dishware into food. Luckily, I only have about an hour before my friends come and pick me up for lunch. Jesus, however, was in the zone, but having fasted for so long, he was incredibly hungry and, probably, incredibly weak.

The point of the fast was to connect with God. Jesus was about to launch into the most incredible, most difficult season of his life culminating in his death and resurrection. He knew he had to have God's agenda and priorities in order to succeed[8]. So, Jesus uses the ancient discipline of prayer and fasting to help "hot-sync" himself to his Heavenly Father.

[8] Are you having a hard time wrapping your mind around Jesus' perfect mix of 100% humanness and 100% divinity? Don't worry. You're in good company. Many faithful Christian scholars and practitioners have struggled with the concept of the Nature of Christ for two millennia. The way I look at it is this, the Creator of the Universe is much more complex and unique than religion, science or I could ever understand (and rightfully so). So, faith allows me to believe in something that I haven't completely figured out yet. Heck, I still can't figure out how my favorite TV show travels via invisible waves from broadcast towers to my TV antenna but that doesn't stop me from watching it every week.

Then, while at his weakest point, Satan shows up tempting with this taunt: "If you really are God's son prove it. Turn these stones into food…you know you're hungry!" It's a great tactic. Satan uses physical need laced with pride to entice Jesus to break his fast. The "prove it" part of it alone would have tripped me up, never mind the play on hunger. Yet, despite the devil's devious approach, Jesus hunkers down and deflects the temptation by quoting from the playbook, so to speak. Jesus uses Deuteronomy 8:1-3, a reference from the Old Testament (or the Torah if you have a Jewish background). It's helpful to know that because they lived in an oral culture (no copy machines, printing press, etc.), most people would have memorized large portions of the Old Testament. So, Jesus would often just quote a small bit of a verse knowing that the listener would know what came before and after the snippet. In this particular reference, God encourages his people to follow his lead and not give up despite what their stomachs may be telling them. By quoting from Deuteronomy, Jesus is relying on one of God's promises instead of taking a handout at Satan's prompting.

Unsuccessful on the physical need front, Satan's second temptation is aimed right at Jesus' ego. Notice how he picks up on Jesus' defensive strategy and adjusts his offense accordingly. This time, Satan uses a Bible reference to try to trip up Jesus. Satan strategically quotes from Psalm 91, a beautiful piece about God's unfailing love. The passage poetically declares God as the perfect protector who will rescue his loved one from the most perilous situations. No harm, the psalm states, could ever come to the one God loves. Satan uses this psalm to needle at Jesus' ego by attacking his position and relationship with God. Basically Satan is saying, "If you really are the Son of God, then prove it. Jump off. The Bible says that God promises to rescue you, that is, if you really are his Chosen One". You can almost hear the malicious tone of voice.

I don't know about you but for me, those are fighting words. I would have almost instantaneously yelled, "Oh, yeah?" and leapt off. When I put myself in Jesus' shoes, I immediately feel a swelling of my pride that wants to scream, "Hey, buddy, you picked the wrong guy to mess around with. I'll show you." But Jesus keeps his cool. Despite his hunger and fatigue, he stays on course. He doesn't even flinch. He rises to the occasion, blowing off Satan by saying something like "Take off, hoser, I'm not falling for that. It also says…" Then Jesus quotes a snippet of Deuteronomy 6 that would bring to mind the few verses before and after it. In that reference, God is basically saying, "No need to follow and serve false gods and no need to put me to the test, I'm a good God and it will go well with you if you follow my lead." With this comeback, Jesus is saying that he doesn't need to prove anything to anyone but just to follow God's lead. Talk about grace under pressure. I'd love to have that perspective all the time. Think of how less stressful life would be if we lived like that day in and day out. I can imagine Satan thinking "Dang! What do I have to do to trip this guy up?"

Seeing that Satan can't make any headway on the physical need front or the ego front, he decides to attack Jesus' emotions; more specifically, he preys on Jesus' potential fears. Think about this for a moment. Jesus was taking this 40-day retreat just before he launches his public ministry. At this point, Jesus knows the game plan. He knows he's the fall guy and that his life on Earth culminates in the ultimate "taking one for the team" on the cross. To put it even more casually, Jesus knows that once the ball starts rolling, it won't stop until he's thrown under the bus of divine justice. That has got to be weighing heavily on his mind at this point. This is precisely where Satan focuses the last temptation.

This time, Satan doesn't waste time fighting with Bible verses. He sends his temptation in the form of a vivid visual, showing Jesus "all the kingdoms of the world and their splendor." Imagine what that might have looked and felt like. To help us relate, picture the mayor or town manager of your city or town driving you out to the best piece of property that your area has to offer. For me, writing in a coastal town 20 miles north of Boston, that would be a new construction, three-story waterfront home on an acre-plus of land with its own private beach and dock. What would that prime property look like in your town? Now, imagine the mayor or town manager waving the title to that property in front of you and saying, if you'll just do this one thing, all this property will be yours to keep. Think of how much fun you and your family or friends could have there. I don't know what the 'this one thing' would be for you, maybe denying your faith, or saying you love the Yankees; something you might consider doing quickly with your fingers crossed, while no one was looking. Now, ratchet it up a thousand fold until one piece of property becomes "all the kingdoms of the world and their splendor" and you see how visually enticing the offer would be.

The 'this' in Jesus' case might just be more valuable than the stunning visual. The 'this' is not simply to bow down to Satan but to short circuit God's plan, be crowned as king right now before any ministry, and AVOID the cross! In effect, the devil is trying to ruin Jesus' entire mission by promising him all the benefits up front without having to lift a finger or sacrifice a single hair on his head. Satan is bribing Jesus to throw the game in exchange for all the wealth and power he can fathom WITHOUT any sacrifice. It's an ingenious temptation. If we look back at our local property scenario, it's like saying you can have the best piece of property and you can quit the family business, never having to work another day in your life. Can you begin to see how cunning this temptation was? I'd like to think I could resist it and prevail, but I'm afraid that reality would find me sipping a fresh cup of Dunkin' Donuts coffee from the porch of my new waterfront home.

Did Jesus buckle under the promise of wealth and, more importantly, fall for the "easy out" from the cross? Not for a moment. Jesus quotes to Satan from Deuteronomy chapter 6 again. He uses verse 13 which, if read together with the three previous verses, points out God's promise of the good life to those who follow his lead alone. Strike three, Satan, you're out! Unlike my Tour de Lowell tribulation, Jesus' Dirty Water mindset allowed him to muster up enough willpower and inner strength to overcome three seriously intense temptations that would have ended everything for Jesus before it ever began.

To me, Dirty Water is definitely more than just a catchy theme song for Red Sox nation. It points to that Bostonian attitude that allows the Sox to muster up victories like the 2004 ALCS against the Yankees and the 2007 ACLS against the Indians where they were on the brink of elimination from 3-0 and 3-1 deficits. It's that same, stick-to-it, don't give up, don't give in mindset that Jesus uses to help him overcome the temptations, resistance, roadblocks, and ceaseless adversity along the way to the cross. Minus the out of place 2011 and 2012 seasons which I'll address in chapter 7, the Red Sox have historically "Loved that Dirty Water." Jesus has too.

EXTRA INNINGS:

1) On a scale of 1 to 10, how strong or weak is your Dirty Water mindset?

2) Name a time when you either benefited or could have benefited from that kind of thinking?

3) What surprises you most in Jesus' determination to accomplish his mission?

4 THE DEVIL WHERES PINSTRIPES:
Jesus' ongoing rivalry with the Yankees of his day

"Feeling like a victim of New York tabloid journalism, Red Sox closer Jonathan Papelbon was incensed that his pregnant wife was the recipient of harsh insults and threats during Tuesday's All-Star red carpet parade down Sixth Avenue in Manhattan.

"I feel like I needed to be in a bullet-proof car," said Papelbon, who was so upset during his session with the media that he used more than a dozen profanities over the course of four minutes. "My wife is pregnant and she's getting her life threatened. It's stupid."[9]

This excerpt was taken from a MLB.com article posted after the 2008 All Star game held at Yankee Stadium. In what normally is a very festive and celebratory atmosphere, the New York media had Red Sox closer Jonathan Papelbon

[9] Quote taken from Papelbon takes media to task Red Sox closer infuriated about back page of Daily News By Ian Browne / MLB.com

seething. "What happened?" you might ask. Although I can't be unbiased no matter how hard I try, the gist of the story is this. In an interview with the media in New York the night before, Papelbon mentioned that he would love to be the American League closer for the All Star game, though he knows Mariano Rivera, a Yankee, should be the closer. It was a statement that, when kept in context, actually honored Rivera. Unfortunately, the back page of the New York Daily News read, "PAPELBUM! Red Sox reliever says he, not Mariano, should close tonight's All-Star Game." To say that Yankee fans do not need any incentive to boo Boston participants is an understatement. When this article hit the press it caused a spike in the ire and venom of the New York fans.

The insults spread from Papelbon to every Red Sox player and staff member, including Sox manager Terry Francona, who was also the American League All-Star team manager. The craziness of the situation came to light whenever a Boston player stepped to the plate. For most of the game, the National League was ahead by two runs. The American League just could not score. Yet, even with home field advantage for the World Series on the line, Yankee Stadium would erupt in boos when a Red Sox player was at bat. Only once did those boos turn to cheers--when J.D. Drew ripped a two-run homer into right field to tie the game. Still, as Drew testified after the game, the fans were back to heckling him in right field when the inning was over and the AL took the field again.

Why this loathing of everything Boston during the 2008

All-Star game? You don't have to be a longstanding Red Sox fan to know about the always simmering rivalry between the Sox and the Yanks. In fact, I don't think you could be a baseball fan anywhere in the country and not be aware of the animosity. Every sports team has a rival but the Red Sox and Yankees' relationship take it to a whole new level. When you see Red Sox Nation newborn babies wearing "Yankees Suck" Onesies, you know it's more than just friendly competition. For most members of Red Sox Nation, the number one obstacle to a World Series title is not the best National League team but the New York Yankees. To Red Sox Nation, the Devil wears pinstripes and hell is fashioned after the old Yankee Stadium. As a kid growing up as a Red Sox fan, I simply learned to dislike the Yankees. It wasn't until I was a bit older that I could understand and appreciate why.

All the research in the world can't come up with a single reason the rivalry is so bitter, but most agree that the history can be traced to the very troubling blunder that Red Sox owner Harry Frazee made back in 1919 when he sold Babe Ruth and several other players to New York for $125,000 cash and a $300,000 loan. Boston had won the World Series title the year before but after that trade they would go on an 86-year championship drought. It was a huge turning point for a ball club that was very successful to that point (5 World Series and 6 American League pennants). The player acquisition was also a huge turning point for a lackluster Yankee club (0 World Series and AL Championship titles). During the rest of Ruth's career, the Yankees would reach the World Series seven times and win four of them. All in all, during the Red Sox's 86-year World Series drought, the Yankees won 26 World Series championships and 39 American League Pennants! For Boston fans the season after season reminder of the tide-turning trade of Babe Ruth to New York perpetually added fuel to the fiery rivalry between the clubs. In fact, prior to the Red Sox winning 2004 World Series, signs, t-shirts, and chants referring back to the 1919 trade and the Curse of the Bambino were commonplace whenever Boston showed up at Yankee Stadium.

The infamous trade of 1919 aside, other factors that make conditions ripe for such an intense rivalry include: the proximity of Boston and New York; the competitiveness of the two cities in culture, tourism, economics, education, and almost every other area of societal life; and the fact that both teams compete not only in the AL but also in the same division, the AL East. One more reason for the rivalry that most often goes unnoticed by sports writers and fans alike is the power of story. That's right, the power of story.

Everybody loves a good story. Whether it is in the form of a movie, a novel, a sitcom, a play, or just in a conversation between friends, a good story hooks us. We'll spend good money to go to the movies to see the most exciting new stories out there. We rent stories from Netflix, buy stories in stores, and borrow stories from libraries. Why are the creation, promotion, and distribution of stories such big business? It's because of the power of story. Without the power of story Hollywood would not be on the map, Shakespeare would be just another dead guy, gossip would be nonexistent and the Yankees-Red Sox rivalry would be nothing more than everyday sports competitiveness.

What makes a story powerful? The power of story lies in its five main ingredients: setting, characters, conflict, climax, and resolve. You can't have a story worth sharing without these five powerful ingredients. They are essentially the ingredients of our everyday lives--where we live, where we work, the friends we hang out with, and the things we do for fun are all there. These five parts of a story communicate a message where belonging and meaning are conveyed as the main characters try to resolve a story's conflict. Before you check out and say "boring," see if these things don't resonate with you.

Story helps us create meaning and belonging. Let's take belonging first. If you have a heartbeat then you have a need for belonging. Relationships, being part of a small community of some sort, no matter what shape or flavor that takes on, are a defining element of the human race. To be human, to some extent, is to want to be included and feel you belong. This works out in all kind of ways. Inner-city street gangs, soccer moms at Starbucks, guys at the bar, skateboarders, sports fans, musicians, church goers, fishing buddies, shopping gals, everyone has a built-in need to be accepted, to be liked, and to belong. This need is so strong that about the worst punishment our prison systems can devise is to withhold the meeting of this need through "solitary confinement."

One of the favorite Red Sox Nation sitcoms of the 80's and 90's was the TV show Cheers. The theme song for this social comedy had these lyrics,

"Where everybody knows your name, and you're always glad you came. You want to be where you can see, troubles are all the same. You want to be where everyone knows your name."

What a great expression of our need to belong. You can probably see now how this is going to tie back in to baseball rivalries, but hold on. Let's talk about meaning and conflict before we get there.

By meaning, I'm getting at purpose, significance, counting for something, having a lasting impact. As I write this chapter, the news has been filled with the outlandish goals of a Chicago-based architectural firm to design and construct the world's tallest building. Apparently, the Royal Family of Saudi Arabia will not be outdone by their counterparts in Dubai who currently own the record for the tallest building on the planet. This new project will be 500ft taller than Dubai's skyscraper reaching up some 3,280 feet. That's the equivalent of two Willis Towers in Chicago (formerly the Sears Tower), currently the tallest building in the U.S. Now there's really no practical reason to erect a building that tall. In fact, it's pretty impractical. Elevator cables do not stretch long enough to reach the top of the proposed building. So a "sky lobby" will need to be constructed so people heading to the top can connect to other elevators that serve the top half of the building. Constructing a building that tall is simply an ego trip. The Royals Saudis want to own the tallest building in the world. As a human race, we feel compelled to excel, to make a mark, to make a difference, to matter, so we are in a continual pursuit to prove ourselves whether by trying to be the biggest, best, fastest, or most successful, or by trying to contribute in some smaller but just as definitive way. The pursuit of meaning may not be as noticeable in all of us until an opportunity to compete or compare presents itself.

There are other ways the basic human need for meaning reveals itself. Sometimes it works out in things like service to a cause, volunteerism, and generosity. Giving, serving, volunteering, or in other words, making a difference are all ways our need for meaning can find fulfillment.

When you combine our human need for belonging and meaning with the catalyst of conflict, you have the making of a good story. Meaning and belonging are what hooks us into a story and what makes us relate to the plot and characters in the story. That's why the epic movie Titanic was so immensely popular. We could identify with the characters and their struggle. We were pulling for Jack, the lower class Irishman, and Rose, the upper class, rebellious teenaged British girl. The movie sucked us into the story and meaning and belonging pinned it to our hearts. Once the movie was over, you really felt like you were part of the experience. The storyline was so powerful that I remember hearing on the radio that one woman had been to the movie 18 times!

Sports have these same elements of story. Team affiliation is a common way we find belonging among friends and family. It can even be something that defines a bit of who we are. I have to confess that I have an uncle who, for as long as I have known him, has been a Green Bay Packers fan. This may not seem strange, except for that he lives deep in the heart of New England Patriots territory. Being the only Green Bay fan I ever knew as a kid, his Packer loyalty seemed almost un-American. My uncle's preference for the Packers was a part of his identity.

Belonging is shown when we affiliate with a team and meaning kicks in the deeper we follow and root for them. So, in any sport, when a rival team plays on your home turf (conflict), more is at stake than just a win or a loss. Diehard fans from both teams have an intangible emotional investment. As fans, we will be more emotionally up or down depending on the final score, than we should be, given that it's just a game. For example, I think most of New England was in a depressed slump for at least an entire week after the Patriots' Super Bowl loss to the Giants (the first time). In a last moment, come-from-behind, crazy helmet catch Giant victory, an undefeated team found itself losing the only game that mattered and also took the joy out of many fans. I remember asking myself a week and a half after that Super Bowl loss, "What is wrong with me?" I knew it was just a game that had no real bearing on my life, but for whatever reason, it felt the same as if I had just been dumped by a girlfriend who I thought was The One. Why did I feel that way? Because of the power of story embedded in sports.

Combine the power of story with a historically seated, venomous rivalry such as the Red Sox and Yankees and you have the makings of news reports like the one opening this chapter. The setting and conflict of this rivalry turbocharged with meaning and belonging has made for many memorable moments in baseball history and will continue to do so, as long as all the elements of story persist. Without the power of story phenomena at work in the hearts of every human being, the rivalry between Boston and New York would be no big deal. Yet, because the power of story is maxed out in this rivalry, normal, everyday people change into the sort who would issue a death threat to the pregnant spouse of an opposing player![10]

Rivalries are by no means limited to the realm of sports. As I already pointed out earlier, Jesus had a serious rivalry going on with the Pharisees, the religious leaders of his day. And this rivalry is every bit as intense and venomous as the worst moments of the Red Sox/Yankees rivalry. This seems a bit counterintuitive, doesn't it? You'd think Jesus would have gotten along fine with religious people of his day. That's not the case at all. In fact, this rivalry would become so heated that it would eventually end with Jesus nailed to a cross!

There's an incredible story that really helps you put your finger on the pulse of Jesus' rivalry. It comes from chapter 11 of the book of John, another of the four gospels (or biographies) of Jesus' life, message, and work.

Picture this: It's spring time in Bethany, a unique village nestled just outside of Jerusalem at an elevation of about 2,000 ft. The weather is teetering between cold and rainy one day and warm and sunny the next. The wild flowers are in bloom and their fragrance fills the mountain air. Bethany is

---

[10] Rivalry has one weakness: reconciliation. NY Yankees singing Sweet Caroline after the April Boston marathon bombings and Boston fans honoring of the retirement of Mario Rivera are two huge elements in telexing the intensity of the 2013 season's rivalry.

the last outpost on a long, difficult trek from the surrounding lowlands up to Jerusalem. The village was not only a sight for sore eyes for weary travelers on their way to Jerusalem but it was also a rare place of refuge and care for the sick, hurting and poor of Jerusalem. In fact, the name Bethany literally means "house of misery" or "poor house" because many of its inhabitants were in dire need physically, financially, or both. Archeological remains suggest that there was even a leper colony residing in the village.

There's good evidence that among Bethany's miserable were a thriving group known as the Essenes. The Essenes were a communal group of people dedicated to disengaging from the excesses of society and championing the cause of the poor, sick and outcast. It's believed that Mary, Martha and Lazarus, siblings who are among the main characters in this story, were part of this community and committed their time and their wealth to its success. We don't know much about the source of Mary, Martha and Lazarus' wealth, but it's evident they were generous, compassionate, and in very good standing within the community. In Red Sox Nation terms, they are the Johnny Peskys of their village. They would have been frequent recipients of MLB's Roberto Clemente award. It's no wonder we find Jesus frequently showing up in Bethany to visit these three friends who do a great job living out the message he has been communicating.

Here comes the conflict. Lazarus, the younger brother of the trio becomes sick and, after a couple of days, he dies. Mary and Martha tried to speed word to Jesus, but by the time he makes his way to Bethany, Lazarus has been dead for four days.[11]

The scene is very moving. The tragedy of the death of "one of the good guys" brings out many friends and supporters to Mary and Martha's home to comfort them. News quickly travels to the sisters that Jesus is (finally) coming up the road. Here's a piece of the story from John chapter 11:

"Now Bethany was less than two miles from Jerusalem, and many Jews had come to Martha and Mary to comfort them in the loss of their brother. When Martha heard that Jesus was coming, she went out to meet him, but Mary stayed at home.

"Lord," Martha said to Jesus, "if you had been here, my brother would not have died. But I know that even now God will give you whatever you ask."

Jesus said to her, "Your brother will rise again."

Martha answered, "I know he will rise again in the resurrection at the last day."

Jesus said to her, "I am the resurrection and the life. The one who believes in me will live, even though they die; and whoever lives by believing in me will never die. Do you believe this?"

"Yes, Lord," she replied, "I believe that you are the Messiah, the Son of God, who is to come into the world."

After she had said this, she went back and called her

---

[11] The Bible indicates that Jesus actually takes his time on purpose! He lets his disciples know that he wants to make sure Lazarus isn't just 'mostly dead' like Wesley in the Princes Bride but undeniably, dead as a doornail.

sister Mary aside. "The Teacher is here," she said, "and is asking for you." When Mary heard this, she got up quickly and went to him. Now Jesus had not yet entered the village, but was still at the place where Martha had met him. When the Jews who had been with Mary in the house, comforting her, noticed how quickly she got up and went out, they followed her, supposing she was going to the tomb to mourn there.

When Mary reached the place where Jesus was and saw him, she fell at his feet and said, "Lord, if you had been here, my brother would not have died."

When Jesus saw her weeping, and the Jews who had come along with her also weeping, he was deeply moved in spirit and troubled. "Where have you laid him?" he asked.

"Come and see, Lord," they replied.

Jesus wept. Then the Jews said, "See how he loved him!" But some of them said, "Could not he who opened the eyes of the blind man have kept this man from dying?"

Jesus, once more deeply moved, came to the tomb. It was a cave with a stone laid across the entrance. "Take away the stone," he said.

"But, Lord," said Martha, the sister of the dead man, "by this time there is a bad odor, for he has been there four days."

Then Jesus said, "Did I not tell you that if you believe, you will see the glory of God?"

So they took away the stone. Then Jesus looked up and said, "Father, I thank you that you have heard me. I knew that you always hear me, but I said this for the benefit of the people standing here, that they may believe that you sent me."

When he had said this, Jesus called in a loud voice, "Lazarus, come out!" The dead man came out, his hands and feet wrapped with strips of linen, and a cloth around his face. Jesus said to them, "Take off the grave clothes and let him go."

Therefore many of the Jews who had come to visit Mary, and had seen what Jesus did, believed in him. But some of them went to the Pharisees and told them what Jesus had done. Then the chief priests and the Pharisees called a meeting of the Sanhedrin[12]. ~ *New International Version,* John 11:18-47

Amazing story, huh? First, Lazarus, a great person and good friend of Jesus, passes away. Then Jesus shows up four days too late. Then Jesus, in front of the whole crowd, raises Lazarus from the dead!

But the even more amazing piece of the story is that in solving the conflict of Lazarus' death Jesus actually begins another conflict--a conflict that will turn out to be the climax to his own story, quickly leading him to be falsely accused, arrested, wrongfully condemned, and executed in one of the most public, painful ways. How does such an amazing miracle like bringing back Lazarus from the dead turn into a conflict? Did you catch the last two lines of the Bible reading?

---

[12] Sanhedrin is the term for the Jewish high council. It was a very powerful group!

"But some of them went to the Pharisees and told them what Jesus had done. Then the chief priests and the Pharisees called a meeting of the Sanhedrin."

The public display of Jesus power and authority brought the rivalry between him and the religious leaders to the boiling point. Instead of saying, in light of this miracle we are being informed of, "maybe Jesus is really the Son of God," they essentially said, "Jesus' popularity is getting too big, let's snuff him out before it gets any bigger!"

In chapters two and three, I talked about this rivalry's main ingredients. They can be boiled down to the topic of who is in God's favor. The religious leaders of their day said that only good, moral people like themselves could ever think about approaching God. After all, God is perfect and holy, the Creator and Sustainer of the universe. God doesn't hang around with the riff-raff of the human race. To the Pharisees, riff-raff included anyone and everyone who didn't outwardly appear to having their act together, whether morally, emotionally, physically, or financially.

Jesus' central message was the polar opposite. He taught that because of what he was doing, God is accessible to everyone. No one, no matter how emotional, physical, spiritual or financially banged up they are, no one is far from God; not only that, but God actively seeks them out!

So when Jesus raises Lazarus from the dead it pretty much seals his doom. How can you debunk the claims of Jesus if he's raising people from the dead in front of massive crowds? The miracle in Bethany was a watershed moment where either you were going to believe or hunker down and refuse to believe. The latter is exactly what the religious chose. Despite the testimony of many from Bethany and Jerusalem, including Lazarus himself (whom the Pharisees were also thinking of killing so they could erase proof of the miracle), the Pharisees, priests, and elders decide to arrest and kill Jesus at their earliest convenience.

Writing this last paragraph made me wonder if there are things that I refuse to be open about as a church leader. I hope and pray that I am humble and honest enough to never be so blatantly closed-minded about anything the way the religious leaders were about Jesus.

EXTRA INNINGS:

1)   What has been your role in the Yankee/Red Sox rivalry?

2)   What are your top five movies? Can you see the power of story at work in those films?

3)   If you were a religious leader back in Jesus' day, is there anything that could have helped you be open to the claims of Jesus? Would that help someone consider Jesus today?

5 REVERSING THE CURSE:
The day that changed history

Much has been written and filmed on that legendary 2004 American League Championship Series victory—the one where, for the first time in sports history, a team comes back from a 0-3 deficit to win a seven-game series. Every baseball fan (and every New Englander regardless of their interest in baseball) knows the gist of this unbelievable, history-making series. I don't pretend to think I could possibly add further insight or intrigue to what's already been published, filmed or broadcast about the greatest sports comeback. Instead, I want to highlight the key "power of story" ingredients that got stirred together perfectly to form one of the most potent sports stories ever. If, in 2004, you step into the shoes of any of the players or new manager Terry Francona or put yourself in the seat of any diehard Red Sox fan, you'll see how incredibly gut- wrenching, debilitating and humiliating the near sweep by the Yankees would have been...and almost was.

The Setting: No, Not The Yankees Again!

Coming off the painful 2003 ALCS loss to the Yankees, where defeat was snatched from the jaws of victory when Grady Little decided to let Pedro Martinez keep pitching into the 8th inning of Game 7, the Red Sox once again had to get past the Evil Empire (as Larry Luchino had dubbed the Yankees) to reach the World Series. But it was much more than just facing the Yankees again. The Yankees represented 86 years of trying hard but coming up short. It represented 86 years of "We're going to do it this year," only to again be named the losers.

If you're a Red Sox fan and have forgotten the misery, or if you're reading this book as a baseball (or Jesus) fan and never have been part of Red Sox Nation, then let me give you a non-baseball example to help you feel the "hopeful hopelessness" that every Red Sox fan 18 and older was feeling that October. The feeling would be akin to your wedding day, a long awaited, long planned for day to mark a new and joyous beginning. The problem is, you have been engaged several times before and each time, inexplicably, your fiancé has bailed at the last minute, leaving you standing alone at the altar, facing a bewildered gathering of friends and family and the tears of your mother in the front row.

The Red Sox had come so very close to winning baseball's ultimate reward in 1986. Just a handful of outs away from breaking the curse, only to have their first baseman commit a Little League mistake, letting a routine ground ball skitter between his legs. 1946, 1967, and 1986 were all Game 7 World Series losses.

In the five years leading up to 2004, Boston had faced New York twice to punch their ticket to the World Series. Each time they went home early, leaving the team's and the fans' hopes dead on the field. So here we are again, Red Sox vs. Yankees in the 2004 American League Championship Series. Could it possibly happen this year? Could we dare hope after last year or '99 or (flinch) '86? Yes. Maybe this is the year. Yes, this could be the big one! I hope I don't get left at the altar.

The Characters: "We're just a bunch of idiots"

If you were to line up the Boston Red Sox and the New York Yankees players side by side, the clean cut, clean shaven, tidy Yankees would make the untucked, long haired, bearded Red Sox look like characters in the movie Old School rather than professional baseball players. It's neither exaggeration nor cruelty to say that Johnny Damon looked like the Geico caveman, Manny Ramirez looked like he was wearing baseball PJ's when he would untuck his baggy uniform, Bronson Arroyo had better cornrows than fields in Kansas, and Pedro Martinez looked like his cap was about to burst apart from all the black curly hair stuffed under it. But what these guys did have was talent and heart, and they were coming off a smoking hot end run (42-18 since August 1). Their appearance nevertheless invited you to doubt the moment they slipped a little. It was this general vibe that led Damon to dub his team "The Idiots."

It's also important to know that at end of July '04 there were major trade activities. The Red Sox management wanted to upgrade their defense to match their potent offense. The key figure in those trades was the most beloved Red Sox player to play during his eight year tenure with Boston (1997-2003), Nomar Garciaparra. Nomar was a first round draft pick in 1994, won the Rookie of the Year Award and the Silver Slugger Award in 1997, and had five trips to the All Star game during his time with the Sox. Famous for his great bat and his quirky and superstitious batting routine, Nomar batted .357 in 1999 and .372 in 2000! Unfortunately, wrist surgery had sidelined him in 2001 and while still hovering a bit above .300, Nomar's defensive skills took a bit of a hit. He committed six errors in his first 37 games in 2004. On July 31, Boston shocked Red Sox Nation fans by trading Nomar for Gold Glovers Orlando Cabrera and Doug Mientkiewicz. Orlando would replace Nomar at shortstop and Doug would be a backup first baseman. Also worth noting, the Red Sox made a much smaller, seemingly less significant trade for outfielder Dave Roberts.

The Conflict: Yankees Lead 3-0

The setting is the 2004 ALCS. The characters are the self-dubbed Idiots pitted up against the star-studded New York Yankees. The conflict appears in the pathetic way the Red Sox dropped the first three games of the series! Curt Shilling, one of the two Red Sox aces in the pitching rotation got shellacked in the opener at Yankee Stadium, leaving the game down 6-0 after just three innings. Pedro Martinez took the mound the second night and pitched well but gave up a two-run homer in the sixth. The Sox lost again 3-1. Game 3 gave Boston a fresh chance with the Red Sox returning to Fenway Park. Did they take advantage of the home field crowd? No, they silenced the crowd with poor pitching that resulted in a 19-8 loss, the worst in the series.

What happened to the Fenway Faithful and Red Sox Nation fans around the country after those first three losses? The terrible start had a polarizing effect. For a large number of fans who had been left at the altar by their team far too often, they seemed to anticipate it; the third loss at Fenway just kicked them into premature defeatist thinking. If you watch news footage and interviews from after game three you'll hear statements like, "Yeah, we're the big choke" and even more painfully put, "I can't believe I fell for it again." Boston Globe writer Dan Shaughnessy labeled the Red Sox a "Pack of Frauds" in his article published the day after their third loss.

Criticizing the naysayers for their lack of faith is easy in hindsight, but history was on their side. The big fact cited in every news report, every article published, and every conversation at the local Dunkin' Donuts was that no team in the 100 plus year history of baseball ever came back from a 0-3 deficit. None! The way the Yankees were playing, the hope of winning even one game was bleak. Winning four games in a row was downright ludicrous, even for the most diehard Red Sox fan. I don't for a second blame anyone who braced for the terrible fall that should have occurred.

On the other side of the spectrum were the fans who absolutely refused to concede the series. Despite the facts, despite the legend of Babe Ruth's curse, despite historical fact, these fans continued to believe. Their incredible faith in their team had one sole argument in its favor: "We don't have to win four games in a row, we only have to win this one game, and we'll take it game by game." In theory they were right. The Red Sox only had to win Game 4 but then they would have to win Game 5 and 6 and 7. Though valid, the argument sounded ridiculous to anyone outside their never-say-die camp.

The Climax – "Don't Let Us Win Tonight"

This was exactly what Kevin Millar told every player, coach, reporter and staff member before the start of Game 4. Several sources, including Terry Francona's biography Francona: The Red Sox Years and ESPN's 4 Days in October (part of the 30 for 30 series) cite Millar repeatedly saying, "Don't let us win tonight... we got Pedro on the mound tomorrow, then Schil... Don't let us win tonight!"

Would they win Game 4? Were there signs of the bride on the church premises? If you were to tune in at the middle of the ninth inning of Game 4, you would say, "Sorry, not this time!" The Yankees had a slim but certain 4-3 lead, and over the loud speaker came those two dreaded words, "Mariano Rivera". The Yankees were playing great baseball and they had just sent in the best closer in baseball history. Mariano Rivera had a 0.69 playoff ERA (That's little more than half a run every nine innings he pitched!) at the time he walked across the outfield and onto the mound to seal Boston's fate. The Red Sox were only three outs from being swept. Three outs!

As Red Sox fans donned rally caps and prayerfully held up "We Believe" signs with their fingers crossed, Kevin Millar worked a rare walk from Rivera, and then came probably the most famous steal in baseball history. Francona pinch-ran speedy Dave Roberts for Millar. Everyone watching the game that night knew Roberts was going to try to steal second base. Before even throwing a pitch to Red Sox third baseman Bill Meuller, Riviera threw over to first base three times trying to pick off Roberts, who was taking as big a lead as he could. That's when the magic began. Despite a great throw down to second from Yankees catcher Jose Posada, Dave Roberts managed to steal the base. That was the pivotal moment in the game and the series. Next, Bill Meuller hit a groundball single to centerfield scoring Roberts and tying the ball game. Game 4 continued on into the next day and around 1 a.m. the Red Sox broke the tie with a David Ortiz two-run, walk-off home run! New York had failed to slam the door shut on the Sox that night and handed them one more chance to stay alive.

Game 5, the last game of the series to be held at Fenway, would turn out to be the longest playoff game in MLB history. With about as much drama and excitement as any baseball game could possibly contain, the Red Sox went on to win in the 14th inning with Ortiz, once again, coming through, this time with a walk-off single. The Yankees let

Boston win that night, too, and the series would move to New York for Game 6.

In retrospect, Game 6 may actually be the game with the most hype of all the playoff and World Series games that year. It was the infamous 'bloody sock' game pitched by Curt Schilling. The old Yankee Stadium was rocking with 56,000 crazed fans. Babe Ruth/Curse signs we're everywhere. The big news was that Schilling had injured himself in his start against the Anaheim Angels, tearing the stabilizing sheathing that surrounds the ankle tendon. The injury was most likely the main contributor to Schilling's awful Game 1 start. The day before the start of Game 6, the Red Sox team doctor put three stitches into Curt's ankle, temporarily securing the loose tendon to deep tissue. The series outcome was resting on the effectiveness of this minor surgery and Schilling's pitching (remember, he gave up six runs in three innings in Game 1). Much to every Yankee fan's chagrin, and Red Sox fan's elation, Curt pitched fantastically. Unbelievably, Schilling pitched seven innings giving up only one run on four hits! The Sox would win Game 6 with a score of 4-2.

Now, Kevin Millar's "Don't let us win tonight" warning seemed prophetic. Just a few nights ago, the Red Sox appeared as hopeless and lifeless as Lazarus, four days after they placed him in the tomb in Bethany. Yet here they were, in Game 7 of the American League Championship Series at Yankee Stadium!

It may not have been as thrilling as the Game 4 and 5 nail biters, and it didn't have all the hype that Schilling's injury brought to Game 6, but Derek Lowe's pitching performance in Game 7 was every bit as outstanding. Lowe pitched otherworldly, allowing only one hit and one run over six innings with only 69 pitches! In any other playoff series this would be the highlight and Lowe would be in line for series MVP but in light of the incredible heroics on the field and at the plate, it was just one of many unbelievable moments.

The Red Sox went on to win Game 7, in a very undramatic fashion when compared to the earlier games. In the first inning, Manny Ramirez hit a two-run homerun and then in the second, Johnny Damon hit a grand slam! The Yankees never had a chance. The Red Sox finished with a 10-3 victory. History was made. The curse was broken. The bride actually walked down the aisle this time.

The Resolution –Everything has changed!

I'm not sure which fan base was more shocked; Boston or New York. New York, the perennial winners, were now experiencing what was a normal feeling for Boston fans: the left-at-the-altar agony of defeat. For Boston fans, no matter if they had full belief, mixed belief, or unbelief before the incredible comeback victory, now there was a unified sense of confidence. It was as if the ALCS was the World Series and the real World Series would be just some sort of exhibition type, celebration series. Despite having to face the St Louis Cardinals, who had won 105 games that season and was the team that defeated Boston in Game 7 of both the 1946 and 1967 World Series, Red Sox fans knew they were going to win hands down. Their intuition proved right. The Red Sox would go on to sweep the St. Louis Cardinals, never trailing once in the entire four-game affair. The 2004 Boston Red Sox were the World Series Champions for the first time in 86 years!

As I finish up this book, nine years after the 2004 victory, it's hard for me to express how much everything has changed. With Boston's 2007 World Series Championship, the "left me at the altar again" feeling has vanished without a trace! Now there's a bold expectation to win all the time. Honestly, I am still basking in the glow of the 2004 season, let alone the 2007 season. In fact, after growing up through the later part of an 86-year, seemingly unquenchable World Series drought, it still seems impossible to me that the Red Sox actually won two World Series in a four years span. I still remember as a 13-year-old budding fan, the punched-in-the-gut feeling that came when Bill Buckner committed that infamous error in the '86 World Series. Yet I seem to be the exception to the rule. A new air is continuously blowing in Boston. Armed with two World Series Championships and helped along by the three Super Bowl titles, an NBA Championship title, and a Stanley Cup, Red Sox Nation is decidedly in a new chapter. No, a new era!

Red Sox Nation has been transformed! We won't let setbacks like '11 and '12 meltdown seasons slow us down (see the last chapter for more on this). We've developed an appetite for winning. The bride came down the aisle and the ceremony was spectacular, the reception was great, and the honeymoon was so fantastic it will never end! In Red Sox Nation, everything has changed!

It's such an incredible baseball story that I even find non-sports fans interested in it. Setting, characters, conflict, climax, and resolve are all there in colorful, passionate fullness. The 86-year drought, the bunch of idiots losing the first three games, the history-making come from behind victory, and the World Series sweep are incredibly powerful ingredients to a legendary story. But they are only that powerful, the story only so captivating because of a deeper, much more profound, and much more impactful story that is still playing out: the story of the human race. The more we understand this bigger story and the more we are able situate the smaller stories of life into this bigger story, the more we can appreciate that the overarching story of human existence and the stories like the 2004 Red Sox World Series run which are merely little pieces of that big story. Let me explain.

It is right here where the big idea of this book as introduced in 'Chapter 1: God and Baseball' finds its focus. Why do all these smaller stories matter to us? Why do we have such an insatiable appetite for story? Why do our hearts stir us to the point where we jump out of our seats and clap and cheer at a ball game or shed real tears as we sit in the movie theater watching a story being projected onto the screen attached to the theater wall? Because we, ourselves, are in the middle of this bigger story. Our lives make up pages and chapters in this incredible epic story of human existence. Our lives, our smaller stories, are pieces of this massive narrative. God, the Creator, is the author. We are some of the characters, and our life situation is part of the setting. If you look at this bigger story of life through the lens of the Bible, you'll find just how remarkably similar the conflict, climax, and resolve is to the 2004 Red Sox season; just played out on a much wider, grander scale. Let's look more closely at this story we find ourselves in.

The Setting – Not the way it's supposed to be.

If you were to ask most anyone over the age of 18, "Do you think the world is the way it's supposed to be?" You'll probably hear a thousand different descriptions of why things are not the way they are supposed to be. Political, economic, financial, and ethical failures of all sizes and shapes would most likely be mentioned. But it wasn't always this way.

Try this exercise with me for a moment. Imagine rewinding human history back towards the very beginning of the reel, back to the Garden of Eden. It's a picture of paradise. Relationally, economically, environmentally, and spiritually, it is a perfect place.

There are no smoke stacks, no leaky mufflers, no chemical dumping. There is no pollution. Nature is in a perfect symbiotic relationship with human beings. Humans tend to and care for their environment – there are no slash and burn techniques; no deforestation, nothing in danger of extinction. In return, nature supplies all that people need for life and more. The beauty is breath taking. The work of caring for creation is a labor of love; bringing satisfaction and pleasure to those entrusted to care for it.

In this place, you'll find no unemployment offices, no welfare lines, no homeless shelters or food pantries. In fact, there is not even a trace of inequality. There are no-haves and have-nots because everyone has all they need to be abundantly satisfied. There is no want!

The quality of this place is incredible. You won't find any discount shops or irregulars racks or generic brands. Everything is premium because nothing is rushed, no corners are cut. Work here is art, and every product and service rendered is a masterpiece.

Relationally speaking, it doesn't get any better than this. There is perfect peace. No crime, no poverty, no corporate scandals. No one is abused, marginalized, or otherwise taken advantage of. Words that describe the social aspect of life here include trust, intimacy, joy, contentment, pleasure, respect, and complete satisfaction. No matter how hard you look, you won't find hypocrisy, self-centeredness or exclusion. Loving and being loved are the main activities. People are vulnerable to one another because there is absolute trust, total transparency, and no shame.

Some people might be happy to find out that there are no churches here. Not because there is no faith, worship, or God, but because there is no religion! There are no standards or limitations on how or where we can express faith. Why? Because all of life is God's and the creation story is about his involvement in our lives! God is not an abstract set of beliefs or a cosmic judge or a distant life force. In this place, the creator is both holy and loving, both almighty and personal. People here follow God's design for life because they know God is completely good and perfectly just. They trust their Creator because they have experienced personally his trustworthiness.

Sounds good, doesn't it? That's how Genesis, the first book in the Bible, describes the start of human existence. In the opening two chapters of the Bible, the Creator declares [my paraphrase], "That turned out pretty good!" on six different occasions. But one time, God changes his assessment from "good" to "Now, that's very good!" Why the upgrade in superlatives? Believe it or not, it's because of you and me.

The Characters – A bunch of potential

The story of life starts with God, and then we quickly find out that God's story is written for us. If God is the subject of the story, then human beings are the direct object. Unlike Johnny Damon's self-description, "a bunch of idiots," the Bible lets us know that God sees us very differently. God places us at the head of his creation as his business partners; to protect and serve, sustain, and continue his creating work. To help us along in this partnership, God creates us in his likeness, filled with amazing potential.

We are created with great capacity to be good, to do good and to create good. The image of God is detected in the human race when people design skyscrapers, when a mom delivers and nurses her baby for the first time, and when personal wealth is used to start a school and hospital for people with no access to either. The image of God shows itself when we exercise compassion, when we give our time and energy to the aid of others, and when we care for and foster the potential of God's creation around us.

Then, get a load of this. When God had finished creating us and commissioned us as partners in the business, he stepped back and said this is "very good." God's very good creation is given to us, his very good people.

But even better than being made in God's image, even better than being in charge of all of creation, is that we were created to know God. Notice these verses from Genesis chapter three:

> Then the man and his wife heard the sound of the LORD God as he was walking in the garden in the cool of the day... the LORD God called to them, "Where are you?" ~ *New International Version*, Genesis 3:8-9

Can you imagine that the first human interaction we see with God is God taking a walk in the garden in the late afternoon hoping that Adam and Eve would join him? It's a very innocent picture. It's a very intentional picture. Genesis goes out of the way to show God's personal, relational nature. He may be the author of everything in existence but he wants to be in relationship with his people; as intimate a relationship as three people taking an afternoon walk together on a crisp fall day. We were created by God and for God.

The Conflict - Evil leads the series 3-0

The conflict arises when in the beginning of chapter 3 we read a scenario that has recurred a zillion times throughout human history. It's a story where human beings, the creation, think that the Creator is holding out and is setting up rules to limit them and keep them under his thumb.

The story goes like this... God gave the man and woman everything under the sun. They could use any part of creation they wanted. They could eat from any fruit or vegetable bearing plant they wanted. They had the whole run of the place except for two trees at the very center of the expansive area called Eden: the tree of knowledge of good and evil and the tree of life. Those were the only two things, among tens of thousands of fruit and vegetable bearing plants that were off limits. That's a restriction percentage of way below 1% of creation. So what do you think the two humans do? They start hanging around the off limit trees until they convince themselves that God is holding out and decide to try some fruit from the tree of knowledge of good and evil.

It went down exactly like when a parent says to a young child "Don't touch the handle of that pot; it is very hot." And the child, wanting to exert his own will, wanting to know the experience his mother is keeping him from, reaches out, touches the pot and is badly scalded.

God's says "Stay away from this tree, when you eat from it you'll know evil. " They chose to do things their own way. They don't listen; they give God the old "I can handle my life myself, I don't need your simple rules" line, and they reach out and eat. When they do, they open themselves up to everything God stands against. In swallowing the "I know better than God" bite, the two humans come to know evil and all its possibilities. No sooner than the bite hits their stomachs do they feel for the first time guilt and shame. They begin a cycle of selfishness and sin that will soon spiral out of control and lead to blame shifting and betrayal, and eventually to jealousy, rage, murder, envy, and every other kind of ugly thought and action that leads us further and further from "the way it's supposed to be." From that moment on, this Paradise Lost story gets replayed over and over again in every conceivable situation and circumstance.

Genesis chapter three is the setting for the story of the human race; very good creation, pure intimate relationships, marred by selfishness, envy, ego and mismanaged desire. Daily we, the creation, have declared we know better than the Creator and again and again we find out that we are wrong. Our innocence has been lost, our souls have been marred, and creation has been twisted. To save us from remaining in this state of imperfection, God evicts the humans from the Garden, so they can't eat also from the tree of life and remain in that condition permanently. The perfect peace and pleasure that humans have had among themselves and between them and God becomes, well, not the way it's supposed to be! The new score is evil one, people zero.

I often wondered as a kid, "Why didn't God just make us a little more like robots so we only could choose good? Why didn't God create us so that we could never choose selfishly or out of jealousy or greed?"

The truth is, if we didn't have freedom of choice, if we didn't have our own will, we wouldn't be made in God's image. There wouldn't be community or sincere relationships or love without choice. And there you have it. In order to have the perfect design, in order for God's creation to be "very good," God had to create us with the possibility to choose the not so good. In order to experience intimate love and trust, God had to create us with the ability to break trust and be unloving... but I'm getting off track. Let's get back to our story.

So, just after the boat sets sail, there is guilt and shame, lust and murder, envy, jealousy, greed, and every other kind of pain and suffering that we inflict on each other and on ourselves. We live in a world where adultery is a social norm, where the human race spends $13 billion on pornography. We live in a world where classmates waste their potential on drugs and alcohol, where bullying, racism, exclusion, hate, jealousy, greed, lying, selfishness, and self-righteousness abound. We live in a messed up world, and sometimes we and our families are a mess.

Is there any hope for us?

If you were God, what would you do at this point in the story? How would you remedy the fact that things have gone so off track and things are not the way they are supposed to be? What if you were the one to come up with the plan to restore life back to the way it was intended? How would you do it? Could you find a way to hit the reset button? Even if there were a reset button, would that work? No, our hearts would still be bent towards selfishness, jealousy and ego. We would still do things our own way, thinking we're smarter than God, and we'd still be stuck in the mire of our own "sin."

You couldn't just hit the reset button. You would have to win people over. Now remember there is no technology, no TV's, no radios, not even newspapers. So you're incredibly limited.

You would want to gather as many people as possible. You would want a high level of commitment and buy-in. You would need a high level of trust and cooperation. You would need to influence every sector of life: families, corporations, governments, economies and nations. Twitter and YouTube would have been invaluable, but they won't be invented for another few millennia.

Interestingly enough, God kicks off his rescue strategy in the very same way he kicks off creation: within a small family. He decides to use families as the vehicle for implementing his Rescue Plan. Incredibly wise in many respects, families have the potential to contain more unity and commitment and trust than any corporation or government structure or NGO ever could. A family of two can multiply incredibly fast. You start with a husband and wife they have 5, 6, 7, + kids (remember there was no birth control back then) those kids have a few kids, and in one generation you have gone from 2 to 30. Then to 70 and then 180 and then it starts to go viral and in short order a family becomes a tribe, then several tribes then a nation. The family is an incredibly fast and effective way to pass down values and stories of faith and a worldview for living. God chose to begin to reverse the tide of everything gone wrong with creation through a network of families that explode in number until they eventually become a nation!

But, if you're familiar with the Bible you know that the rescue team falls prey to the same mistakes as everyone else and slowly the rescue team drifts not only away from the rescue game plan but also away from God, the giver of that game plan. Things get ugly, and the people of God drift so far from God's game plan, they absorb every unhealthy, destructive practice going on in the world around. Eventually, the Rescue Team itself is in desperate need of rescue. The series is now evil two, people zero.

But all hope isn't lost! God had a back-up plan in mind right from day one: Jesus! Let me stop again and ask: If you were God and you were going to enter into your creation somehow, how would you do it? Would you enter as a king or maybe as a military commander? I asked my two young sons this question, and one of them replied: "I'd come as a Ninja warrior!"

God could have chosen any method. He decides instead, keeping to form, to enter into a small family, ironically, as the weakest member of that family, a little baby boy. That boy would grow up and influence his family circle, his community circles and then go on to start another circle--a circle of 12. As a rabbi (a respected teacher on faith and life), Jesus poured his all into these guys. Through sacrifice and service, and through an incredible demonstration of power and humility, compassion and courage, Jesus showed those 12 and the world a radically different way of life: A way of strength, shown not in control, but in love. A way of influence, not shown in ordering people around, but by bringing out the best in people. A way of deep contentment and satisfaction not marked by materialism or greed, but by generosity and gratitude!

It looks like evil might just lose game three, but wait. Remember Lazarus in Bethany from chapter four? Remember "Jesus' popularity is getting too big, let's snuff him out before it gets any bigger"? Jesus would go on to lose game three much like the Red Sox got pummeled by the Yankees in Game 3 of the 2004 ALCS at Fenway Park. The situation unraveled very quickly!

The Climax – Did God Make A Mistake?

You wouldn't think that God would write the betrayal, arrest, suffering and crucifixion of the Rescue Hero into his Rescue Plan for the human race! If you thought Grady Little's mistake of leaving Pedro in too long in 2003 was bad, this twist in the Rescue story is disastrous! Surely God didn't intend it to play out this way… or did he?

At first glance, the plan doesn't seem to make any sense! Why in the world would God set things up this way? Why would the Creator of the universe, the sustainer of all existence inflict suffering, humiliation, pain and death on himself? It's the same answer to the question why did they Red Sox have to face the Yankees in the ALCS? The answer, of course, is so they could beat them.

We already alluded to the answer when we talked about Jesus entering his creation not as a king, general, or a John Wayne gunslinger but as a helpless infant born to a poor traveling couple. This is the key piece to puzzle. This is the key focus of the Rescue Plan. God doesn't just want to free his creation from the effects of all its collective bad choices, no God wants to free his creation to hear his call back to the way things are supposed to be. God is dying, literally, to woo his creation back to original partnership he had with them. A partnership where we continue the creating and sustaining work in a way that blesses rather than curses, a way that loves rather than hates, gives instead of grabs, a way that looks out for others and not just self-propels. So the God of the universe becomes the ultimate model of this way of life. He clothes himself with humanity and is betrayed and abandoned. He suffers at the hand of injustice. He is falsely accused but is silent. He is wrongfully convicted but goes quietly. He is violently abused but turns the other cheek. He is condemned and crucified for nothing he has done. He lays aside power, privilege and status and is judged to set his creation free. In suffering and dying on the cross, Jesus takes on sin and judgment and death and absorbs it into himself. It's the ultimate symbol of love. But it doesn't stop there. It can't stop there!

One of my favorite quotes from the broadcast of the infamous Game 4 in the 2004 ALCS came from Joe Buck after Kevin Millar got a leadoff walk against Mariano Rivera in the 9th inning. As Millar drops the bat and begins to trot down to first base Joe quips, "And there's life for the Red Sox." The moment in time marked the beginning of "reversing the curse." For the Rescue Plan and the Rescue Team, that moment came early Sunday morning, two days after the brutal events that landed Jesus crucified, dead and lying in a tomb.

Two women, both named Mary, were first to arrive at the

tomb where Jesus was laid. After the crucifixion, the religious leaders asked the Roman authorities to post guards at the tomb so no one would try to steal Jesus' body and claim he rose from the dead. So the authorities had a massive stone rolled in front of the tomb entrance and then posted two guards to keep an eye on it. Just as the ladies arrived, the Bible says, the ground shook and they saw an angel "whose appearance was like lightning and whose clothes where white as snow." The angel rolled back the stone and then sat on it. "Don't be afraid! I know you're looking for Jesus. He is not here; he has risen, just as he said he would. Take a look in for yourselves," the angel tells the frightened women. The guards were so afraid they fainted. The Bible goes on to say the women, mixed with both fear and joy, ran back to tell Jesus' disciples, friends and followers. And there is life for the Rescue Plan!

Just like much of the highly skeptical commentaries, news articles and conversations in New England after Game 3, there was a huge amount of skepticism in the bewildered Rescue Team. Jesus' closest friends and followers didn't believe the reports that Jesus' was alive. After all, they saw with their own eyes, Jesus arrested and crucified. They were standing nearby when they took his dead, tattered body off the cross. No matter that Jesus gave them a heads up about how this was going to happen, the visceral, heart wrenching evidence that his time was over outweighed any hope whatsoever. Despite the skepticism, the reality was true. All hope was not lost. Evil did not win. The prison door of human nature or sinfulness, or whatever else you want to call our bent towards mucking things up, was blown open because Jesus was not dead but alive! The rescue plan is on, but now it's unstoppable.

The Resolution – Everything has changed!

Let's look at one more Bible reading that will give us the last piece of this puzzle:

On the evening of that first day of the week, when the disciples were together, with the doors locked for fear of the Jewish leaders, Jesus came and stood among them and said, "Peace be with you!" After he said this, he showed them his hands and side. The disciples were overjoyed when they saw the Lord.

Again Jesus said, "Peace be with you! As the Father has sent me, I am sending you." And with that he breathed on them and said, "Receive the Holy Spirit." ~ John 20:19-22

What difference did Jesus' death and resurrection make? All the difference in the world! It allowed God to go from abstract concept to internal reality. It moved God from out there somewhere, calling us, inviting us, to right up with us and unbelievably in us.

Among a million other things that happened that first Easter weekend, there was a cosmic transaction that took place on the cross and was made public the following Sunday. Before I state what it was in "faith" terms, let me first describe it in ordinary life terms.

Let's say you had this brilliant idea for a small business.

You are so excited about it and committed so much to it that you convinced the biggest bank in town to loan you $3 million! You take the money and buy some office space, get all the equipment you need to make this idea happen, and then you go public. You expect it to be incredible, for sales to start pouring in. The exact opposite begins to happen. You have some small sales and a few newspaper mentions but you can't even pay the bills. You quickly realize that not only is your dream not going to be realized but that you are now on the hook for $3 million. You quickly do the math and figure out that you have to pay approximately $8,300 per month for the next 30 years! Let's say that there's no such thing as filing for bankruptcy; you are on the hook for this. You can pretty much kiss any hopes of enjoying life goodbye!

Then some mysterious benefactor comes in and doesn't just completely pay off your debt so that you're completely free from creditors; he goes a step further. He then links your freshly cleared checking account to his own personal checking account—one with an unlimited balance!

This is a ludicrous example but this is the best analogy I can give for the transaction that took place on Easter. Jesus, who is God squeezed into his own creation in human form, comes preaching and practicing a different way. Then he does the unthinkable, he gives himself up for us. On the cross, Jesus picks up our collective debt for all the ways that we have gone against God's designed and contributed to the "not the way it's supposed to be" status. Jesus picks up the tab for all the times we have essentially said to God, "'I can handle my life myself, I don't need you," but then have gone on to hurt ourselves and others with our greed, apathy, jealousy, self-centeredness, ego,... fill in the blank with any of your latest regrets.

But the transaction does not stop there. Jesus didn't just forgive us and say "Don't do it again!" No. He forgives us and then connects our account with his account. He smashes the religious legalistic treadmill of having to "be good" in order to be in good standing with God. He breaks the false religious pattern that many of us grow up in that if we do good God then God likes us, but if we do bad God dislikes us. It's a major shift from "let's follow God so that he loves us" to God loves us and is with us, so let's follow him into this incredibly rich way of life.

What ends up happening is that we go from thinking that life is about me, that my story is the biggest, most important story (which always ends up in disaster) to my story takes on more wholeness and wellness and purpose and meaning when I let God's story infuse and take over my story. His story of good triumphing over evil, love over hate, generosity over injustice, becomes alive and drives our story.

Do you see now why the 2004 Red Sox season was so special? Do you see why the 2004 ALCS was so captivating? Because it hit the sports chords of this "come from behind, underdog, victory has been squelched, death has seemingly vanquished life once again, all hope is lost component" of the Rescue Plan. It's the same song but hummed to a happy baseball tune.

This Rescue Plan song is seen all over the place. The ending to the widely successful Lord of the Rings trilogy is a mini replay of it. So is the climatic fight scene in Star Wars: Return of Jedi, when Luke Skywalker is saved instead of killed by his father Darth Vader. It's played out when Jack saves Rose by giving her the floating plank while he remained in the freezing water. You see it in the climax to the movie The Matrix when Neo takes on the agents and absorbs them and their bullets to save his friends and the human race. I could go on and on to show you how there are whispers and echoes and min-replays of the gospel story all over creation. It's in art, music, movies, fiction and non-fiction. It's everywhere, including in baseball.

EXTRA INNINGS:

1.   What is your favorite movie of all time? Can you see the good versus evil, love wins, the underdog pulls off the victory theme?

2.   Where are some other places you have found this theme in life?

3.   Where does your story fit in relation to God's bigger overarching story?

6 LIVING WITH A BOSTON ACCENT:
Pahking the cah in Havahd Yahd

I had a very strange experience when I attended graduate school at Gordon-Conwell Seminary in South Hamilton, MA. Even though the school was located about 20 miles north of Boston, most of the faculty and student body were from out of state. Texas, North Carolina, California and many Midwest states were among those represented. So when I started getting picked on for the way I pronounced my words, I was surprised. After all, the school is in New England; I should not be the one who feels out of place.

One of the most memorable moments of people not understanding me because of my accent came when I was spelling my last name for a professor. I said "Laird... L, A, I, R, D."

He said, "Sorry I caught L, A, I, what was the next letter?" The conversation continued as following:

Me: "R! (which sounded to him like 'Ahh')"
Prof: "What?"

Me: "R" (emphatically)

Prof: "What?" (exasperated)

Me: "R, R, R" (very emphatically w/ gestures)

Prof: (silent with a very perplexed look on his face)

I said emphatically, "You know 'Q, R, S'?"

"Oh!", he said. "Oh, you meant 'R'!"

I left that conversation half smiling, half thinking, "What's wrong with these people?"

After being married to a Midwesterner for over sixteen years and being more conscious about my accent as a public speaker, I have greatly toned it down. Still, it's not strange for me to have someone point out how I say a certain word or even point out the word choice itself (like 'bubblah' instead of drinking fountain or 'sneakahs' instead of tennis shoes or 'down cellah' instead of in the basement). If you live in or near Boston long enough, you're bound to pick up an accent. A little lilt here or there, a missing or additional consonant here or there; little things that sort of set you apart from everyone not from Boston.

The same dynamic holds true once you start living out God's Rescue Plan. You begin to pick up a different "accent." The more you dive in and embrace faith as a way of life, the more pronounced your accent will become. Why? Simply because you are not living on autopilot anymore. Instead of going with the flow and giving in to human nature, you are now trying to follow God's lead intentionally. So when someone wrongs you, instead of writing them off and burning the relational bridge, you choose the harder path and try to resolve the issue. When you're coming up with a budget, instead of just factoring in spending and savings, you make a line item called generosity, so that you can be help someone in need or support a worthwhile cause. When you have to make a difficult decision, instead of asking which option benefits you the most, you actually pray, "God, do you have any thoughts on this?" and wait to see if you get a nudge before you continue your thinking. When you live life following God's lead for any long period of time, you will pick up an accent that will seem both odd and refreshing. Living with an accent is often contagious to others, although there will always be some who may don't understand you and poke fun at your intentional living. Still, that's no reason not to embrace this freeing accent.

There are two very powerful moments in recent past of Red Sox Nation that embody this idea of living with an accent. The first came about during opening day at Fenway Park in 2008.

The ultimate sign that the curse was broken (and also an incredible "living with an accent" moment) came when the Boston Red Sox asked Bill Buckner to throw out the opening pitch at Fenway Park on April 8, 2008. It was also the day that Boston would also celebrate its 2007 World Series title. If you didn't catch this moment when it happened, then you need to catch it on YouTube[13].

The moment starts with Joe Castiglione announcing over the loud speaker, "Now it's time to welcome the star who will throw our ceremonial first pitch on this day that we honor

---

[13] In YouTube, search for 'DET@BOS: Bill Buckner throws the out first pitch.'

champions and how happy we are amidst this celebration and joy that this Red Sox alumnus had come back to join us. He has amassed Hall of Fame caliber credentials in his 21-year Major League career and the Red Sox would never have been able to won the 1986 American League pennant without him. Won't you please welcome back to Boston and won't you please let him know that he is welcome always, number 6 Bill Buckner!"

Immediately following this intro, Bill Buckner enters from left field to an incredible two-minute-long standing ovation. Greatly moved by this overpowering reception, Bill wipes his teary eyes several times then throws a strike to his old teammate Dwight Evans. It's clear that Bill experienced the moment as redemptive and restoring. The ceremony closes with this announcement over Fenway's PA system, "Ladies and gentlemen, one of the greatest players to wear the Red Sox uniform and one of the kindest members to be a part of our alumni, thank you again, Bill Buckner!" Once again the Fenway Faithful erupts with loud applause.

This for me was one of the clearest, loudest signs that God can be found in sports. The moment strongly displays many of the Rescue Plan principles that God give us in the Bible: humility to recognize the need and importance to invite Bill back to Fenway, to offer reconciliation of past hurts and letdowns, and a very non-human-nature-like praise of Bill and desire for Bill to feel like a welcomed, celebrated part of Red Sox history. The Red Sox leadership didn't need to do this at all. They could have done it at a less momentous occasion but they chose to do it when the eyes and attention of baseball fans everywhere would be fixed on Fenway. It was an occasion that made many proud to be a fan of the Red Sox organization.

The second moment that exemplifies "living with an accent" happened just after the Marathon Bombings of April 2013. Two terrorists exploded homemade bombs near the finish line of the Boston Marathon, killing three bystanders and wounding hundreds. The terrorists later killed another security officer and wounded others before being apprehended. The surreal feel of being glued to the TV screen and sending and receiving texts from out-of-state friends and family reminded me how I felt during the 9/11 terrorist attacks. The Boston Marathon bombings brought both sadness and anger to Massachusetts residents.

As tradition, during the Monday of the Boston Marathon, the Red Sox had played an 11 a.m. game and had finished up about 40 minutes before the bombings took place. They had prepared for a quick getaway for a game in Cleveland the next day. This is when the Red Sox began "living with an accent."

When the Red Sox' plane landed in Cleveland the team made plans to eat dinner together and brainstorm ways the players could respond and show support for the people of Boston. An amazing 24 players came together that night. That may not seem like a big deal, but if you compare that to the four players that showed up to Johnny Pesky's funeral the previous year during Bobby Valentine's dis-unifying tenure, you'll see how unusual it was. That meeting sparked the creative idea to hang a Red Sox Jersey with the words Boston

Strong and the number 617 (the greater Boston area code) on it from the visitor's dugout at Progressive Field in Cleveland. For the first home game after the bombings, Boston also created and hung a large banner with the Red Sox B and the word Strong underneath it.

While it would have been reasonable to expect the team to have a moment of silence and possibly wear black bands on their uniforms, they went far beyond the expected. That players' meeting led to extraordinary comfort and brought positive meaning to a city so impacted by terrorism. They didn't have to come up with Boston Strong, didn't have to make impassioned speeches and didn't have to win the next four games in a row. But they did. They were living with an accent and it showed in their love, compassion, and desire to bring out the best in Red Sox Nation.

There is a great quote from Irenaeus, one of the Early Church fathers, that says, "The glory of God is men and women fully alive." That is the point of living with an accent. When we take our small stories and let God's big story infuse and guide it, our lives take on a richer, more meaningful existence. We become fully alive. The more we give ourselves to God's greater story, the more we fully embrace the Rescue Plan as a way of life, the more impact, significance, purpose, and contentment we will feel.

So don't worry about people wondering why you're being generous. Don't hold back the desire to bring out the best in an uncomfortable situation. Boldly love and be loved. Boldly serve, reconcile, and renew. If people don't seem to understand you because of your accent, just give 'em a half-smile and half-wonder "What's wrong with these people?"

EXTRA INNINGS:

1.   Do you have any memorable accent stories (on either the giving or receiving end)?

2.   Can you recall a specific time when you have "lived with an accent"? How did it feel?

3.   What are a couple of things that hold you back from "living with an accent"?

7 THE NEWENGLAND SKEPTIC:
And the "Road to Redemption"

One of the things that go along with the Boston Attitude that I described early in the book is a bent towards skepticism. When you Google the word "skeptical," and the definition "not easily convinced; having doubts or reservations," a picture of a New Englander just might pop up. As someone born and raised in greater Boston and as someone who has spent nearly two decades here as a pastor (in the business of influencing others towards faith), I can say without a doubt (are you skeptical yet?), that skepticism is practically an inborn quality among New Englanders. Growing up, if you tried to sneak an opinion or theory by as fact, someone in the family would call you out and then mildly pick on you. I grew up in a culture where you raise a skeptical eyebrow at anything out of the ordinary. If there were some way to measure what topics elicit the most skepticism among New Englanders, I would bet the top two are political promises and religious claims.

To be honest, my role as a pastor doesn't make me any less of a skeptic than other diehard New Englanders. I grew up watching politicians make promises, only to have older adults in my life comment on how laughable those promises turned out to be. I was 15 when Vice President George H.W. Bush, made the promise during his Republican Nomination acceptance speech of "no new taxes." Actually the full quote from the speech is much stronger:

"My opponent won't rule out raising taxes. But I will. And the Congress will push me to raise taxes and I'll say no. And they'll push, and I'll say no, and they'll push again, and I'll say to them, 'Read my lips: no new taxes.'"

Some say, it was this pledge that helped Bush gather enough support among voters from both parties to be elected President. What do you think actually happened once he got into office? To President Bush's credit, he tried to fend off Congress, but in the end he wound up raising taxes.

Growing up in a mixed Irish Catholic/Methodist family, I also was given much reason to be skeptical of religious leaders and their messages. Do the names Jim Bakker (adultery and tax evasion), Jimmy Swaggart (hiring prostitutes), or Ted Haggard (adultery and Crystal Meth) ring a bell? While I'm listing public religious scandals of my lifetime, I can't exclude here the biggest one: the global pedophile scandal and cover up in the Catholic Church. Because of these, and unfortunately, probably, countless more examples, there are plenty of reasons to embrace a skeptical outlook across the board, especially when it comes to politics and religion.

After reading this far, you may be dying to email or text me a big, skeptical question: If what you said about the Boston Attitude and the Dirty Water Mindset is true, why the epic meltdowns and failures of the 2011 and 2012 seasons? Don't those two seasons water down or even cancel out those notions altogether? It's a good question but there's actually a reasonable answer that I hope will satisfy your skepticism. When things go well and life is good, it's easy to forget what got you where you are.

When I was in graduate school, preparing to become a pastor, I remember seeing a sign that hung across the chained up doors of an old stone cathedral. The sign said, "Out of business. Forgot what we were in business for." That sign made a big impact on me. Seeing a building that a once housed a bustling, productive, church whose business was changing lives for the better become an empty structure that would be sold and repurposed into chic urban office condos was jarring. I vowed from that moment on always to ask "What is our vision? Where are we headed? Are we on target?"

If you look back to the above list of religious leaders who have screwed up royally, I bet you could pinpoint a time in each one of their lives when success and status-quo thinking caused a drifting away from the vision, purpose and values that made them thrive in the first place.

As I was writing this chapter, one of the bloggers I subscribe to, Seth Godin, was writing on a similar topic. His October 12, 2013, blog is entitled "Is Google jumping the shark?" "Jumping the shark" is a phrase that originated with the hyped up, unusually dramatic episode of Happy Days where Fonzie jumps over a shark on water skis. The phrase "jumping the shark" was coined by John Hein and originally referred to a movement in the life of a television show that marks a departure from the show's usual content and themes in order to keep attracting viewers. Over the years, the phrase has broadened to refer to "the moment when a brand, design, or creative effort's evolution loses the essential qualities that initially defined its success and declines, ultimately, into irrelevance.[14]" Jumping the shark seems to be the best explanation to the incredible collapse of the 2011 season and the abysmal 2012 season.

A team vision and values shift appears to have caused the Red Sox' 2010 season collapse when they entered September with a nine-game lead and needed to win only eight of their last 27 games. September was a complete disaster! I'll never forget the last two weeks of that regular season.

I had won a Red Sox lottery that gave me the chance to buy two tickets to the American League Division Series to be held at Fenway. Having never attended a playoff game, I was incredibly excited to buy these tickets. I called my dad and told him we were going to the game. I printed out the electronic tickets and left them out to bask in glory on my desk. The thought never, ever entered my mind that we wouldn't make it into the playoffs. In fact, the Red Sox became the first team in MLB history to lose a nine game lead heading into September.

---

[14] http://en.wikipedia.org/wiki/Jumping_the_shark

If you thought, as I did, that the 2011 season couldn't get any worse, you were wrong. The 2011 season took the cake. It was horrible; by far the worst Red Sox season in my four decades of life. The Red Sox finished last in the AL East division with a 69-93 record, their worst season since 1965! Overpaid and underperforming seemed to best describe the team that year.

What caused the monumental collapse in 2011? Why wasn't the organization able to fix it in 2012? The answers to these questions are the same: they lost the vision and values of what made the 2004 World Series Championship team so special. The Red Sox had "jumped the shark" with the signing of superstars Carl Crawford (seven years, $142 million) and Adrian Gonzalez (seven years, $154 million).

In The Francona Years, Dan Shaughnessy writes how the dip in the Red Sox TV ratings sparked a desire among ownership to become "sexier." The Gonzalez and Crawford signings were visible signs of the tangible business versus baseball tension. Don't get me wrong, these two guys are great baseball players but going out and spending premium dollars for two players is more the Yankees' style and less the Red Sox way. It was a move designed to make a more lucrative baseball product.

There were other signs that the Red Sox were losing their "team first, game before ego, we're in this together" mentality. There was a noticeable lack of player unity. Stuff was leaking out to the press that newer would have in years past. Players were barking at other players. The new manager, Bobby Valentine, seemed to anger players and alienate himself from everyone. Pitchers who were not playing were periodically consuming chicken and beer while playing video games in the clubhouse during the game. Looking from the outside, fans could sense something toxic going on inside. The team unity that characterized the 2004 "idiots" was noticeably absent in 2012. Also absent was the effectiveness of a star-studded team that was a World Series favorite in April.

Chicken and beer, players at odds with one another, club house secrets being leaked to the media, a dysfunctional manager were all signs that the team had lost that winning formula: Talent plus work ethic plus commitment to one another and to the game equals winning. The 2011 and 2012 Red Sox went out of business because they forgot what they were in business for. They had jumped the shark.

Because of the historic failures of the 2011 and 2012 seasons, no one, not even the diehard Red Sox optimist, held any real hope of seeing the 2013 Red Sox in the playoffs. Across the board, the Red Sox were believed to be in a rebuilding phase that would take two or three years to take shape. The team had made some offseason moves, picking up good but not great (at least in the eyes of the media) players. Mike Napoli, Shane Victorino, Johnny Gomes, Stephen Drew, and Ryan Dempster were added to the 2013 roster. Why did the front office go after these guys? One big reason, they were not just good players; they were good players who had a track record for both winning and for being great teammates. Would chemistry among good team players be enough for a chance to play in October? The general vibe in the media was no. I heard a commentator for one of the Boston radio networks confess that after all the winter acquisitions he predicted Boston would have a win total in the upper eighties, but after looking at them in spring training, he downgraded his estimate to a win total in the upper seventies.

That negative vibe was not present in the clubhouse. Right from the start of spring training the players came in focused on hard work and winning and there was a noticeable chemistry among all the players, even though so many of them were new to the Red Sox. In interviews with General Manager Ben Cherington and Manager John Farrell, reporters heard full confirmation that a unique winning chemistry was developing. Cherington remarked on several different occasions that he could tell right from week one that this group was different. He cited examples of how even in the cafeteria the players were talking baseball. They were focused on winning and focused on winning together. The "road to redemption" was underway.

It seemed highly unlikely that a team could "un-jump" the shark in one season but's that's exactly what the 2013 Red Sox did. They went from worst place in the AL East in 2012 to World Series Champions in 2013! They blew away all winter and spring predictions. The Red Sox were strong all season long never losing more than three consecutive games during the entire regular season. They came together in the post season and beat out three teams with elite pitching staffs.

How did they do it? What made such a radical shift from

worst to first in such a short time? They got back to that winning formula. John Farrell brought focus and stability where the previous manager had left distraction and mistrust. Gomes, Victorino, Drew, Napoli, Dempster, and eventually Jake Peavy brought a unique competitive spirit--not just a competitive spirit to do their best individually, but a competitive spirit to win as a team. In an interview after an amazing come-from-behind win in Game 2 of the 2013 ALCS series, Ryan Dempster reiterated that this team was amazing in the way everyone looks out for each other and picks up each other. He said, "It's a check your ego at the door team." There were no individual stars but one winning team. The vibe of the 2013 Red Sox team has been the whole is greater than the sum of its parts. Against all odds, the team has found a way to unjump the shark and get back to what they were originally in business for: winning baseball games as a team. Sometimes the skeptic is wrong.

I'd like to push my luck and say we can make the same argument for "living with an accent" (where living with an accent means embracing faith as a way of life and living out the Rescue Plan as given in the Bible). There have been countless times where followers of Jesus have royally screwed up and completely lost their way. The Crusades, the Inquisition, and the Witch Hysteria in 1690 in Salem, MA, are just some of the many examples you can cite alongside the list I mentioned in the beginning of the chapter.

Do these examples mean that there are flaws in the Rescue Plan? Is there something fundamentally wrong with the rescue strategy or rescue team? I believe the answer is no.

The problem lies in us, imperfect people, who can too easily be swayed by power, money, status, and sex. The only real fault you can find with God is in his inviting us to be a part of the plan. It's the skeptical realist in me that thinks this way, but there is another side to it.

When people throughout history have wholeheartedly embraced the way of life modeled and taught by Jesus, things have changed. In his book Who Is This Man? John Ortberg quotes Yale historian Jaroslav Pelikan:

"Regardless of what anyone may personally think of or believe about him, Jesus of Nazareth has been the dominant figure in the history of Western Culture for almost twenty centuries. If it were possible, with some sort of super magnet, to pull up out of history every scrap of metal bearing at least a trace of his name, how much would be left?"

The book goes on to show the immense and immeasurable impact that Jesus' influence has had on improving women's rights, providing education and care for the sick regardless of economic status, founding the concept of the university and higher learning, promoting the end of slavery and so much more.

Without the rescue plan and the Rescue Hero, we'd be sunk. When human beings catch and embrace the rescue plan as a way of life, we partner with God in amazing, life-transforming ways. We partner with God in huge global initiatives like ending world hunger and micro initiatives like loving our neighbor.

I remember a time early in my married life when Laura and I were standing around the coffee machine waiting for that liquid gold to finish brewing. It was early on a cold January morning. As we watched and waited, we heard a peculiar sound coming from the direction of the neighbor's back yard. It was a "chink, chink, chink" sort of sound. It stopped for a moment but then we heard it again, "chink, chink, chink." I looked out the window and saw my next door neighbor, a single woman past the age of retirement, chipping logs out of her frozen wood pile. Mary lived by herself in a big farmhouse next door and heated it with her woodstove. Apparently rain had gotten in and through her firewood and cemented individual logs into one solid block of ice.

I stared at her out the window and said, "Stinks to be her!" That was not "living with an accent" thinking. But Laura, looked at her and said, "Why don't you go down to the hardware store and pick up a few bundles of dried firewood." Definitely, "living with an accent" thinking. Feeling a little sheepish because I, the pastor, should have been the one thinking like that, I made my way to the hardware store and came home with three bundles of dried logs and placed them on my neighbor's back porch.

I forgot about it until later a couple of days later when my neighbor met me in the driveway. She asked me if I had brought her the firewood. I let her know we did and then she let me in on her thoughts. Here's a paraphrase of what she said:

"I can't tell you how thankful I was to see that. In fact, I had such a bad day at work and all I could do was think about how I had to come home and chip out logs from a frozen woodpile. I wanted to cry. I came out of my house and saw the pile and, honestly, I thought an angel put it there; that is, until I saw footprints in the snow leading to your backdoor."

Did you catch that? She actually mistook me for a messenger from God! Why? Because my wife was living out the rescue plan and gave me a good nudge to follow suit.

When we jump the shark and forget why we're in business, we put ourselves in risk of joining the long line of hypocritical people who have lost their way. But, when we embrace faith as a way of life, when we keep in mind why we are here and make our smaller stories about God's bigger story, then we partner with God in changing lives.

I have learned a lesson after that moment of seeing what a difference a small act like buying my neighbor some firewood can make. I learned that I don't want to miss any opportunities to partner with God. I don't want to miss out on writing my story into God's story. And so I start every morning off, before my toes touch the floor, with a prayer. Well, it's more a plea than a prayer, but I start every morning praying, "God thank you for this day. Please help me not to miss you today! Please help me to see what you're doing around me so that I can join you! Amen."

Although the Red Sox may seem like family to you, and their success brings joy across Red Sox Nation, in the end their games are just that; games. All their success, including their World Series sweeps, are just little blips in the history of American sports, which in turn is just a very small category in the rest of word history. Instead of seeing baseball as the end itself, instead of seeing baseball as just entertainment, what if you saw it as another lens through which you can glimpse the Almighty? What if baseball along with sunsets, babies, prime rib, and love are just pointers to help us see the Creator behind his creation? What if baseball is a pointer to help us find and follow God?   If that's the case, then it's worth heading to Fenway!

EXTRA INNINGS:

1.   What are some things you are skeptical of? What could possibly help you overcome your skepticism (certain facts, an experience, etc.)?

2.   What questions would you need answered in order to give faith a try as a way of life?

3.   How would your life and approach to life be different if you temporarily suspended some skepticism to give faith as a way of life a try?

28594846R00069

Made in the USA
Lexington, KY
21 December 2013